Foreword

Dear reader,

Welcome to the first edition of the Homes for Life book of house plans. We trust with our large range of plans available, you may find one to suit both your taste and pocket. Often the most difficult thing in the house building process is actually choosing the dwelling itself and we encourage everybody to look at your chosen site individually and fit a house to it rather than the other way around. This means ensuring fundamental but essential items are not overlooked, for example, the fact that the key living areas i.e. kitchen and dining rooms generally are faced in direction of the key sun areas i.e. south, southwest.

With this in mind, we have devised our system whereby your chosen plan may be reversed to suit the orientation, or indeed the finish may be altered in order to suit the locality or elevation to your taste. We therefore urge you to take the time and consideration into choosing your new home, time well spent which will hopefully lead to many happy years of comfort and enjoyment.

Yours faithfully,

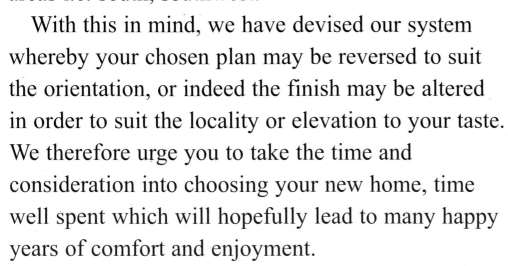

Mark Kelly MASI

Check out the benefits of a Tusa mortgage

At Tusa, we're dedicated to providing you with not just a mortgage, but the right mortgage.
We have made a commitment to all of our customers to provide consistently competitive mortgage rates with no hidden extras and no indemnity bond.
You will also benefit from our unrivalled levels of service, our dedicated personal attention and our longer opening hours. So why not call us today and check out the benefits of a Tusa mortgage.

Call Tusa now on **1850 200 808**
or
Call into Tusa in Superquinn today

www.tusa.ie

tusa
an agent of TSB Bank

PURAFLO Wastewater Treatment

▶ Simple Installation

▶ Agrément certified

▶ Low maintenance and running cost

▶ Protects public health and the environment

▶ Planning advice available

▶ Installation included

Onsite Wastewater Treatment Systems from

BORD NA MÓNA
BORD NA MÓNA ENVIRONMENTAL LIMITED

Phone 1850 381136 for details

ACKNOWLEDGMENTS

Designs:
All designs by Mark Kelly,
Corporate Member Architecture &
Surveying Institute.

Editorial:
Landscaping by Lisa Murphy.
Energy Efficiency by Irish Energy Centre
Insulation tips by Aeroboard

Computer Graphics:
Radius Technologies, Waterford.
Liam Minogue - MK Home Design Ltd.

Printing by:
Kilkenny People Printing Limited.

PUBLISHER

MK Home Design Limited.
22 Upper Patrick Street, Kilkenny,
Ireland.

ACKNOWLEDGMENTS

Mary Dargan, Liam Minogue,
Katrina Mahony, Carol Cantwell.

MK Home Design Ltd.
Homes For Life

CONTENTS

General Information
Planning permission, design alterations, plan prices,
house specifications, and order form 98
As a general guide to room layouts throughout this
publication the reader will find that:

- Entrance/Landing areas - brown
- Kitchen/Dining areas - green
- Living/Sitting areas - blue
- Study/Office areas - magenta
- Bedrooms - brown
- Bathrooms/en-suite/w.c areas - yellow
- Sun room/conservatory areas - orange
- Garage areas - grey

Glenco Ireland Radon Gas Centre Ltd

Glenco Factory Sealed 15WW Foil Reinforced Methane / Radon Membranes.

Glenco Radon Plastic Sumps, Cavity Adapters, universal Top Hats, white Radon Identified Pipe wok, and Accessories for new buildings.

Powerlon 600RM – 1,000 RM Reinforced Geomembrane Liners.

Powerlon Reinforced Perforated roof membranes and super permeable Flame Retardant Breather Membranes.

Powerclad WB insulted scaffold sheeting.

Glenco Ireland Radon Gas Centre Ltd.

Unit 1, Whitelands West, Monasterevin Road, Kildare, Co. Kildare.
Phone No: 045-521110/ 529617 Fax No: 045-522048/ 529618
Website Address: glencoireland.com E– Mail: glencoir@iol.ie

Reverse Osmosis Water Purifier Systems

RO103-TDS
Auto-Flush with TDS Display
Smart Control Box to auto-flush the membrane, build-in TDS meter to know the water quality & membrane's Effectiveness from the LCD Display.

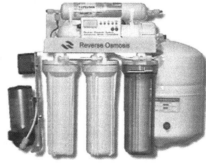

Removes 99% of hard water Contaminants that may be presen In your water: Chlorine, lead, Barium, chromium, Mercury sodium, cadmium, fluoride, nitra calcium, selenium and many mor Household and commercial units For the home, office, pubs, restaurants etc.

For colour brochure and
Advice phone:

Glenco Ireland Radon Gas Centre Ltd.

Phone No: 045-521110/ 529617 Fax No: 045-522048/ 529618

Page 4

A man travels the world over in search of what he needs and returns home to find it.

George Moore (1852 - 1933) Irish writer and art critic.

House A-101

See page 104 to order this design by post.

Floor plan

Hallway	4.8 x 2.2m / 15'8" x 7'2"
Dining Room	3.8 x 3.0m / 12'5" x 9'10"
Kitchen	4.8 x 3.2m / 15'8" x 10'5"
Living Room	5.3 x 3.5m / 17'4" x 11'5"
Study	3.8 x 2.5m / 12'5" x 8'2"
Bathroom	2.1 x 2.2m / 6'10" x 7'2"
Hot Press	1.0 x 1.2m / 3'3" x 3'11"
Bedroom 01	4.5 x 3.5m / 14'9" x 11'5"
En-suite	2.7 x 1.0m / 8'10" x 3'3"
Bedroom 02	3.8 x 3.3m / 12'5" x 10'9"
Bedroom 03	3.3 x 2.4m / 10'9" x 7'10"

AREA

123.5 sq. m. / 1,330 sq. ft.

FRONTAGE

15.3 m. / 50.2 ft.

A hugely popular style of design! The wall between the kitchen and dining rooms may be omitted if desired.

House A-102

See page 102 for plan prices.

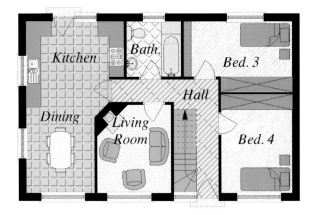

Ground floor plan

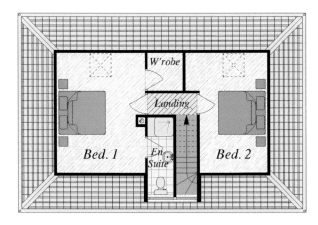

First floor plan

Hallway	4.4 x 1.0m / 14'5" x 3'3"
Living Room	3.4 x 3.1m / 11'2" x 10'2"
Dining Room	3.5 x 2.9m / 11'5" x 9'6"
Kitchen	3.9 x 3.3m / 12'9" x 10'9"
Bathroom	2.1 x 2.3m / 6'10" x 7'6"
Bedroom 03	4.3 x 2.9m / 14'1" x 9'6"
Bedroom 04	3.8 x 3.0m / 12'5" x 9'10"
Landing	2.0 x 1.0m / 6'6" x 3'3"
Bedroom 01	4.9 x 3.9m / 16'1" x 12'9"
En-Suite	3..2 x 1.2m / 10'5" x 3'11"
Wardrobe	1.5 x 1.6 /4'11" x 5'2"
Bedroom 02	4.9 x 3.0m / 16'1" x 9'10"

AREA

120.0 sq. m. / 1,290 sq. ft.

FRONTAGE

11.4 m. / 37.4 ft.

This beautiful dormer provides the privacy and comfort of a house with two stories, together with the economy of a smaller dwelling. Corridor space is deliberately kept to the absolute minimum.

House A-103

Phone 00 353 56 71300 to order plans by credit card from outside the Republic of Ireland.

Floor plan

Hallway	3.5 x 2.1m / 11'5" x 6'10"
Sitting Room	4.6 x 4.0m / 15'1" x 13'1"
Kitchen/Dining	7.5 x 3.6m / 24'7" x 11'9"
Utility	2.5 x 1.7m / 8'2" x 5'6"
Hot Press	1.7 x 1.0m / 5'6" x 3'3"
Bathroom	3.6 x 2.0m / 11'9" x 6'6"
Bedroom 01	5.0 x 3.5m / 16'4" x 11'5"
En-Suite	2.2 x 1.2m / 7'2" x 3'11"
Bedroom 02	3.6 x 3.6m / 11'9" x 11'9"
Bedroom 03	3.6 x 3.6m / 11'9" x 11'9"

AREA
124.5sq. m. / 1,340.10 sq. ft.

FRONTAGE
15.6 m. / 51.2 ft.

Another simple yet popular design eligible for the first time buyers grant. The elongated kitchen/dining provides lots of light and space to this area.

House A-104

See page 102 for plan prices.

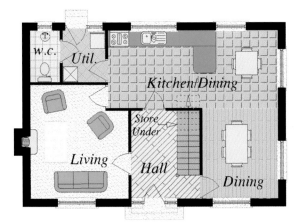

Ground floor plan

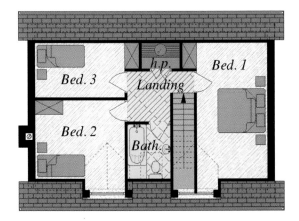

First floor plan

Hallway	3.4 x 2.7m / 11'2" x 8'10"
Kitchen/Dining	6.7 x 3.0m / 21'11" x 9'10"
Living Room	4.4 x 3.9m / 14'5" x 12'9"
Dining	3.5 x 3.0m / 11'5" x 9'10"
Utility	2.0 x 1.7m / 6'6" x 5'6"
WC	2.0 x 1.2m / 6'6" x 3'11"
Landing	2.0 x 1.8m / 6'6" x 5'10"
Bathroom	2.2 x 1.8m / 7'2" x 5'10"
Hot Press	1.6 x 1.1m / 5'2" x 3'7"
Bedroom 01	5.6 x 3.0m / 18'4" x 9'10"
Bedroom 02	3.8 x 3.3m / 12'5" x 10'9"
Bedroom 03	3.8 x 2.2m / 12'5" x 7'2"

AREA
118.6 sq. m. / 1276 sq. ft.

FRONTAGE
10.4m / 34 ft.

Value for money is the key for this exceptionally beautiful, yet practical house. The Georgian effect to the window glazing adds to its appeal.

First Time Buyers Grant

This grant of £3,000 was introduced by the government as an aid to young couples, towards the high cost of building/purchasing their first home. However, strict guidelines have been laid down in order to qualify for such a grant and these criteria are always strictly adhered to:

- The gross floor area shall not exceed 125 sq. metres (1,346 sq. ft.).
- You or your partner may not have previously built or purchased a home inside or outside of Ireland, either together or separately.
- You must live in the house permanently as your normal place of residence.
- The house must be built in accordance with current building regulations and good building practise.
- The dwelling must be constructed by a registered contractor holding a current tax clearance cert./form C2. With "direct labour" type construction, a specified minimum must be completed by a registered contractor as normal V.A.T. registered work. This amount currently stands at £15,000.
- The dwelling must be new.
- Dwellings in many parts of Dublin City and County must comply with specified smoke emission limits for heating appliances. Check with your relative planning authority.

Always bear in mind that it can take up to six months before you receive the £3,000, and is subject to a final inspection. When applying the following must be provided:

- A copy of planning permission with conditions attached.
- Fire safety certificate with conditions attached (only for flats or maisonettes).
- Relevant drawings and specifications.
- Site location map, showing site clearly marked.
- Form NH2B, certificate from inspector of taxes.
- Proof of purchase and/or ownership (this is especially relevant where more than one person is applying).
- A floor area certificate (FAC), where the building has been purchased from a developer/builder. Obviously, this does not apply in cases of self build.

The above data and information should be forwarded to the following address: Department Of The Environment, House Grant Section, O'Connell Bridge House, Dublin 1. Telephone 01-6793377.

Please bear in mind that the information outlined in this page is intended as a guideline solely and if further, more in-depth information is required, please contact the following: Department Of The Environment, Housing Grant Section, Government Offices, Ballina, Co. Mayo. Telephone 096-70677.

In general, it may be assumed that all areas that are "habitable", or are capable of being used, should be included in the aforementioned gross floor area. Areas not included would be "non-habitable areas" such as garages, outbuildings, unused basements etc., etc. In addition, there are some "exemptions" from the requirements as outlined below:

- Maximum floor area - exemptions are available in case of disabled persons.
- Previous ownership - exemptions can be made in the case, again of disabled persons, and also of separated persons. In addition, where a house has been extensively damaged by fire and it is more feasible to construct a new dwelling, exemptions may be allowed.

Please contact your local department of the environment for information and a decision on the above.

House A-105

See page 104 to order plans by post.

Floor plan

Hallway	4.4 x 1.9m / 14'5" x 6'2"
Sitting Room	4.9 x 4.8m / 16'1" x 15'8"
Glazed Area	3.7 x 1.6m / 12'1" x 5'2"
Kitchen/Dining	7.1 x 4.5m / 23'3" x 14'9"
Hot Press	1.5 x 1.2m / 4'11" x 3'11"
Bathroom	3.3 x 3.3m / 10'9" x 10'9"
Bedroom 01	4.9 x 3.3m / 16'1" x 10'9"
En-Suite	3.3 x 0.9m / 10'9" x 2'11"
Bedroom 02	3.8 x 3.5m / 12'5" x 11'5"
Bedroom 03	3.2 x 2.9m / 10'5" x 9'6"
Bedroom 04	3.2 x 2.6m / 10'5" x 8'6"

AREA

125.sq. m. / 1,345 sq. ft.

FRONTAGE (excluding glazed area)

16.8 m. / 55.2 ft.

This spacious family dwelling features a spectacular splayed dining area as one of its main features. If desired, we can add a wall beside the kitchen in order to create a utility space.

House A-106

See page 102 for plan prices.

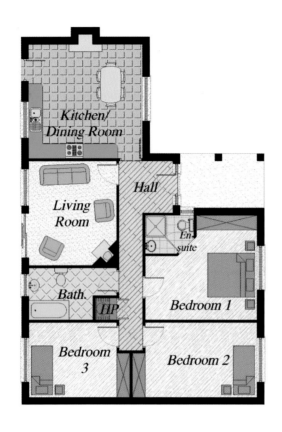

Floor plan

Hallway	2.3 x 2.1m / 7'6" x 6'10"
Kitchen/Dining	4.8 x 4.7m / 15'8" x 15'5"
Living Room	4.3 x 3.7m / 14'1" x 12'1"
Bathroom	2.7 x 2.1m / 8'10" x 6'10"
Hot Press	0.9 x 0.9m / 2'11" x 2'11"
Bedroom 01	4.8 x 4.3m / 15'8" x 14'1"
En-Suite	2.1 x 1.6m / 6'10" x 5'2"
Bedroom 02	4.7 x 3.0m / 15'5" x 9'10"
Bedroom 03	4.3 x 3.2m / 14'1" x 10'5"

AREA

108.4 sq. m. / 1,166.80 sq. ft.

FRONTAGE

10.3m. / 33.8 ft.

Everything required in a family home is included in this compact but elegant design. The exterior provides a great way of including character in a more economical type of dwelling.

House A-107

See page 104 to order plans by post.

Floor plan

Lobby	1.6 x 1.1m / 5'2" x 3'7"
Hallway	2.4 x 1.6m / 7'10" x 5'2"
Living Room	4.5 x 3.7m / 14'9" x 12'1"
Dining Room	4.2 x 2.9m / 13'9" x 9'6"
Kitchen	5.4 x 4.0m / 17'8" x 13'1"
Utility Room	3.4 x 1.8m / 11'2" x 5'10"
W.C.	2.5 x 1.0m / 8'2" x 3'3"
Hot Press	1.7 x 0.8m / 5'6" x 2'7"
Bathroom	3.3 x 2.0m / 10'9" x 6'6"
Bedroom 01	4.5 x 4.5m / 14'9" x 14'9"
En-Suite	3.4 x 0.9m / 11'2" x 2'11"
Bedroom 02	3.9 x 3.7m / 12'9" x 12'1"
Bedroom 03	3.7 x 3.1m / 12'1" x 10'2"

AREA
125.sq. m. / 1,345 sq. ft.

FRONTAGE
16.9 m. / 55.4 ft.

This pretty yet simple bungalow combines an elegant exterior, with a well laid-out and proportioned interior. The position of the separate dining area offers great privacy

While the Building Regulations require that new buildings achieve minimum standards of energy efficiency, higher levels are in many cases worthwhile. Since a house being built today can be expected to be occupied for 60 years or more, an energy-efficient design can yield considerable savings over its lifetime.

Although some energy-saving measures can be implemented at a later stage, retrofitting is often more expensive and less effective than incorporation when the house is being built.

Apart from reducing fuel and electricity bills, an energy-efficient home design can provide improved comfort for occupants while helping to protect the environment. It can also provide insurance against future increases in fuel costs.

This section aims to provide tips on energy efficiency to those planning to build (or buy) a new home. It is not comprehensive ñ the range of details for energy-efficient house design is too wide for that.

FUNDAMENTAL PLANNING DECISIONS

• Site Selection

Energy used in driving from place to place can amount to a significant proportion of a household's total energy consumption. By locating new houses near to work-places, schools, public transport routes, etc., transport energy consumption can be reduced.

Transmission of sunshine through windows (passive solar heating) can reduce heating costs. The selection of a site which is exposed to the low-altitude winter sun can allow for passive solar heating.

By selecting a location sheltered from the wind, heat loss from the building can be reduced. Shelter can be provided by nearby trees, adjacent buildings or surrounding hills. If no such shelter exists, it can be provided in time through planting trees or shrubs.

In some, mainly rural, locations there may be potential for renewable energy sources other than solar; for example hydropower, wind power, wood, biogas, or heat which can be extracted from the ground or sea. The possibility of obtaining heat from a combined heat and power plant or group heating scheme may also influence the selection of a site.

Building form and orientation

A compact building form of minimum surface-to-volume ratio is best for reducing heat loss. However, a rectangular building with one of the longer facades facing south can allow for increased passive solar heating, day-lighting and natural ventilation. As well as reducing energy costs, sunny south-facing rooms also have high amenity value.

Projections such as bay and dormer windows should be kept to a minimum, since by increasing the surface-to-volume ratio of the building, they will increase heat loss. They also tend to be more difficult to insulate effectively.

Pitched roofs should have one slope oriented south to allow for optimum performance of a roof-mounted or roof-integrated active solar heating system. Even if such a system is not planned during construction, it may be installed at some stage during the life of the building.

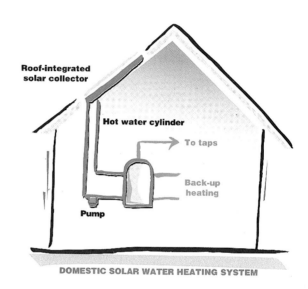

DOMESTIC SOLAR WATER HEATING SYSTEM

Energy assessment

Many decisions affecting the energy performance of a house are taken early in the design process. A method of calculating annual heating energy consumption should be used to compare alternatives at the preliminary design stage.

Permanent ventilation openings result in excessive ventilation in windy weather. Controlled vents should be installed in every room; trickle or slot vents incorporated in window frames can ensure a reasonable amount of continuous fresh air and can be opened up or closed down to a minimum as required.

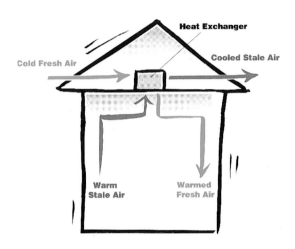

Cooker hoods and small fan exhausts allow for controlled removal of moist air from kitchens and bathrooms, and prevent this air being drawn into living or bedrooms.

Attention should be given, during both design and construction, ensuring that the building is well sealed. Services should be designed with minimum penetration of pipework and cabling through the building's insulated shell. Doors and windows should come with factory-applied draught seals. Porches and draught lobbies can reduce draughts at external doors.

Never seal up a house completely, as a minimum of fresh air is required for health and safety reasons.

If an open fire or other fuel-burning fireplace appliances are to be installed, they should have an independent air supply. This can be achieved by means of an underfloor draught or by using a room sealed appliance such as a balanced flue heater.

A balanced ventilation system involving fans, ductwork and a heat exchanger can transfer heat from warm stale outgoing air to incoming fresh air (this is called 'mechanical ventilation with heat recovery'). Stale air is usually extracted from rooms such as kitchens and bathrooms, and warmed fresh air supplied to living rooms and bedrooms.

For such systems to work well, the house must be well sealed. Correctly sized systems can reduce ventilation heat loss considerably.

If the house is to be built in an area where leakage of radon gas from the ground gives rise to concern, appropriate steps should be taken to prevent its entry into the house. The Radiological Protection Institute of Ireland can advise on this.

Passive solar features

If the house is exposed to the low-altitude winter sun, glazing should be concentrated on the south façade. Window areas on the north façade should be minimised to limit heat loss. Thermal mass within south-facing rooms, e.g. masonry walls or concrete floors, can absorb and store solar energy during the day and release it gradually during the evening. The heating system should have a fast response time and good controls to maximise the usefulness of solar gains. Overheating protection in south-facing rooms in summer can be provided by overhanging eaves, blinds, natural ventilation, thermal mass or other means.

In general, it is not wise to increase south-facing glazed areas too dramatically. Otherwise additional measures will be required to avoid overheating in summer and excessive heat loss at night and on overcast days in winter.

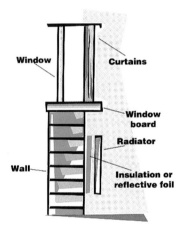

Windows should have a high resistance to heat loss. 'Low-emissivity' double glazing, which has a special coating to reduce heat loss, is recommended. It looks just like ordinary double glazing but has the insulating performance of triple glazing.

Well-fitting curtains can help to retain heat at night. If a radiator is mounted below the window, the curtains should not cover it when closed, but should rest lightly on a window-board or shelf above the radiator. This arrangement will direct warm air from the radiator into the room rather than up behind the curtain.

A well-designed sunspace or conservatory on the south side of a building can reduce the heating needs of a house by acting as a buffer against heat loss and collecting solar energy on fine days. However, there are many examples of sunspaces, poorly designed from an energy point of view, which increase heating requirements. Sunspaces should not be heated, and should be separated from the heated space by walls, and / or closable doors / windows. They should not be regarded as being habitable all year round. The energy losses from one heated sunspace can negate the savings of ten unheated ones!

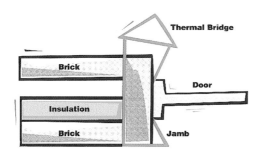

Building materials

The embodied energy of a product is the energy used to produce it, and includes energy used in extracting raw materials, processing and transport, e.g. Irish grown timber will incur lower transport energy use than timber imported from overseas. The embodied energy of a house is typically over five times its annual energy consumption and therefore equates to approximately 5-10% of the total energy consumption during the life of the house.

The building materials selected should have minimum environmental impact during their entire life cycle, including manufacture, use and disposal. Building components should be designed for long life and durability, and ideally should be recyclable at the end of their operating lives.

HEATING SYSTEMS

Energy efficient houses need smaller heating systems than conventional houses. The resulting savings will help to pay for the cost of additional insulation.

Boilers

The heating system should be efficient, not only at full load, but also at lower loads. If looking at oil or gas boilers, you should ensure that the boiler complies with the new EU boiler efficiency directive. In the case of gas boilers, you should consider condensing boilers, which cost a bit more but are highly energy-efficient.

If selecting individual room heaters, consider room sealed, balanced flue units. Room heaters should be correctly sized for the room they are to heat and should be thermostatically controlled.

Hot water systems

It is generally more energy-efficient to heat water using an efficient boiler or other fuel-burning appliance than with an electric immersion heater. The hot water cylinder should be well-insulated; factory applied insulation is generally more effective and durable than a lagging jacket. As well as providing space heating, combination 'combi' boilers supply hot water directly to the taps, thus avoiding the losses associated with storage in a hot water cylinder.

This article was kindly submitted by the Irish Energy Centre. Telephone 1850-376666. www.irish-energy.ie

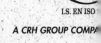

House Designs from 1,351 up to 1,650 sq. ft.

In home-sickness you must keep moving - it is the only disease that does not require rest.

H. de Vere Stacpoole (1863-1931) Irish-born novelist.

House B-101

Phone Lo-Call 1890 713 713 to order plans by credit card.

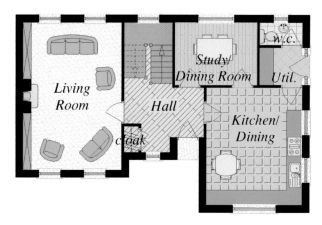

Ground floor plan

First floor plan

Hallway	3.2 x 2.1m / 10'5" x 6'10"
Living Room	5.8 x 4.2m / 19'3" x 13'9"
Study	3.3 x 2.6m / 10'9" x 8'6"
Kit / Din	4.6 x 4.1m / 15'1" x 13'5"
Utility	1.7 x 1.6m / 5'6" x 5'2"
W.C.	1.7 x 1.0m / 5'6" x 3'3"
Landing	4.4 x 1.0m / 14'5" x 3'3"
Bathroom	3.2 x 1.8m / 10'5" x 5'10"
Bedroom 01	4.6 x 4.2m / 15'1" x 13'9"
En-Suite	1.9 x 2.1m / 6'2" x 6'10"
Wardrobe / H.P.	1.9 x 1.3m / 6'2" x 4'3"
Bedroom 02	4.2 x 4.1m / 13'9" x 13'5"
Bedroom 03	5.2 x 3.0m / 17'1" x 9'10"

AREA

143.0 sq. m. / 1,540 sq. ft.

FRONTAGE

12.2 sq. m. / 40 ft.

This well proportioned two-storey shows how well brick and plaster work together in combination. In addition, this tends to lend an impression of width to a dwelling.

House B-102

Phone 00 353 56 71300 to order plans by credit card from outside the Republic of Ireland.

Ground floor plan

First floor plan

Hallway	4.7 x 2.9m / 15'5" x 9'6"
W.C.	2.0 x 1.2m / 6'6" x 3'11"
Utility	2.6 x 1.5m / 8'6" x 4'11"
Kitchen/Dining	6.0 x 3.8m / 19'8" x 12'5"
Living Room	5.0 x 4.5m / 16'4" x 14'9"
Study	2.5 x 2.4m / 8'2" x 7'10"
Landing	3.8 x 1.6m / 12'5" x 5'2"
Bathroom	2.4 x 1.9m / 7'10" x 6'2"
Hot Press	1.2 x 0.9m / 3'11" x 2'11"
Bedroom 01	5.4 x 3.2m / 17'8" x 10'5"
En-Suite	2.0 x 1.6m / 6'6" x 5'2"
Bedroom 02	3.7 x 2.9m / 12'1" x 9'6"
Bedroom 03	3.7 x 2.7m / 12'1" x 8'10"
Bedroom 04	3.7 x 1.9m / 12'1" x 6'2"

AREA
137.4 sq. m. / 1,478.95 sq. ft.

FRONTAGE
9.0 m. / 29.5 ft.

This very well proportioned dormer style dwelling is a spacious family home. The two-story aspect to the front affords full height to the landing and bathroom areas.

House B-103

See page 104 to order this design by post.

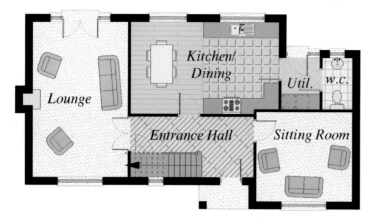

Ground floor plan

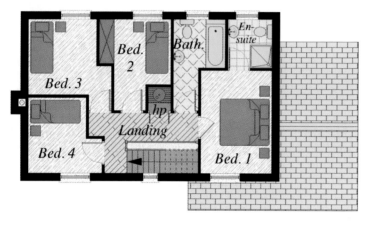

First floor plan

Hallway	4.9 x 2.5m / 16'1" x 8'2"
Lounge	5.9 x 3.9m / 19'4" x 12'9"
Kit / Din	5.9 x 3.7m / 19'4" x 12'1"
Utility	1.8 x 1.9m / 5'10" x 6'2"
W.C.	1.7 x 1.0m / 5'6" x 3'3"
Sitting Room	3.8 x 3.8m / 12'5" x 12'5"
Landing	4.3 x 1.2m / 14'1" x 3'11"
Bathroom	2.1 x 2.0m / 6'10" x 6'6"
Hot Press	0.8 x 1.0m / 2'7" x 3'3"
Bedroom 01	3.9 x 3.0m / 12'9" x 9'10"
En-suite	1.8 x 1.9m / 5'10" x 6'2"
Bedroom 02	3.5 x 2.4m / 11'5" x 7'10"
Bedroom 03	2.9 x 2.9m / 9'6" x 9'6"
Bedroom 04	2.9 x 2.5m / 9'6" x 8'2"

AREA
134.7 sq. m. / 1,450 sq. ft.

FRONTAGE
13.4 m. / 43.9 ft.

One of the more popular designs! The small roof peaks along the eaves add a nice touch of character throughout.

House B-104

See page 102 for plan prices.

Ground floor plan

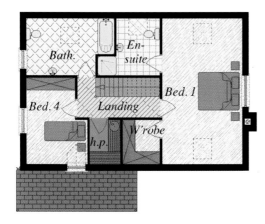

First floor plan

Hallway	1.7 x 1.6m / 5'6" x 5'2"
Kitchen	4.6 x 3.1m / 15'1" x 10'2"
Liv / Din	7.0 x 4.2m / 22'11" x 13'9"
Utility	1.4 x 1.4m / 4'7" x 4'7"
W.C.	1.5 x 1.2 / 4'11" x 3'11"
Boiler	1.0 x 1.1m / 3'3" x 3'7"
Bedroom 02	4.4 x 3.8m / 14'5" x 12'5"
Bedroom 03	3.0 x 2.8m / 9'10" x 9'2"
Landing	3.9 x 1.0m / 12'9" x 3'3"
Bathroom	4.2 x 2.8m / 13'9" x 9'2"
Hot Press	2.0 x 1.6m / 6'6" x 5'2"
Bedroom 01	6.8 x 4.0m / 22'3" x 13'1"
En-suite	2.6 x 2.2m / 8'6" x 7'2"
Wardrobe	2.0 x 1.9m / 6'6" x 6'2"
Bedroom 04	4.0 x 3.1m / 13'1" x 10'2"

AREA

152.8 sq. m. / 1,644 sq. ft.

FRONTAGE

11.1 m. / 36.4 ft.

A combination of American style interior with Irish style, vernacular exterior, which results in this fabulous dwelling. The elegant lines and simple forms provide a very authentic feel.

House B-105

Phone Lo-Call 1890 713 713 to order plans by credit card.

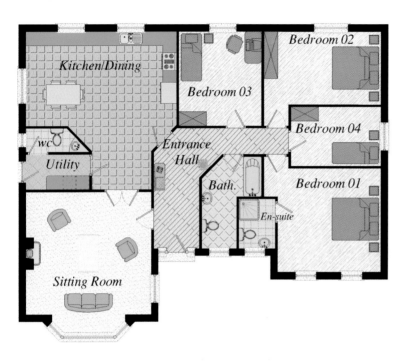

Floor plan

Hallway	5.1 x 2.0m / 16'8" x 6'6"
Sitting Room	5.5 x 5.2m / 18'5" x 17'1"
Kitchen/Dining	6.6 x 4.0m / 21'7" x 13'1"
Utility	2.8 x 1.5m / 9'2" x 4'11"
W.C.	2.8 x 1.0m / 9'2" x 3'3"
Bathroom	3.9 x 1.6m / 12'9" x 5'2"
Bedroom 01	4.5 x 4.4m / 14'9" x 15'5"
En-Suite	2.1 x 1.6m / 6'10" x 5'2"
Bedroom 02	5.1 x 3.1m / 16'8" x 10'2"
Bedroom 03	4.0 x 3.7m / 13'1" x 12'1"
Bedroom 04	3.9 x 2.5m / 12'9" x 8'2"

AREA
153 sq. m. / 1,646 sq. ft.

FRONTAGE
16.2 m. / 52.1 ft.

Here we see how a straightforward single-storey can be transformed into something extra special with a little thought and imagination. The bay window as shown is common in modern day construction, and greatly adds to the amount of light coming into the room.

House B-106

Phone 00 353 56 71300 to order plans by credit card from outside the Republic of Ireland.

Ground floor plan

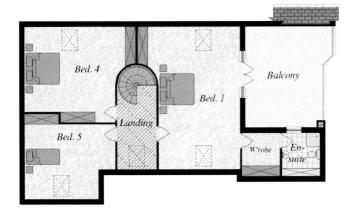

First floor plan

Hallway	3.7 x 3.3m / 12'1" x 10'9"
Bathroom	2.9 x 2.7m / 9'6" x 8'10"
Dining Room	4.3 x 3.3m / 14'1" x 10'9"
Kitchen	4.4 x 3.8m / 14'5" x 12'5"
Utility	2.1 x 1.3m / 6'10" x 4'3"
W.C.	2.1 x 0.8m / 6'10" x 2'7"
Sunroom	2.9 x 2.8m / 9'6" x 9'2"
Living Room	6.4 x 4.6m / 20'1" x 15'1"
Bedroom 03	5.5 x 4.4m / 18'5" x 14'5"
En-suite	2.5 x 1.7m / 8'2" x 5'6"
Bedroom 02	4.4 x 4.4m / 14'5" x 14'5"
Bedroom 01	8.1 x 4.7m / 26'5" x 15'5"
Balcony	5.7 x 4.5m / 18'8" x 14'9"
Wardrobe	2.5 x 2.2m / 8'2" x 7'2"
En-suite	2.5 x 2.3m / 8'2" x 7'6"
Bedroom 04	5.5 x 5.3m / 18'5" x 17'4"
Bedroom 05	5.4 x 4.1m / 17'8" x 13'5"

AREA (Ground floor only)
154.4 sq. m. / 1,661.9 sq. ft.
FRONTAGE
18.0 m. / 59 ft.

This dwelling was designed primarily with the ground floor only in mind, which accommodates everything comfortably. The spectacular upper floor centred around the luxurious main bedroom is an optional extra (naturally we provide plans for both).

Flower Arrangements

Not many things are as decorative or beautiful in the home as flowers. Of course fresh flowers, when they are available would be fantastic anywhere. Although, this isn't always a practical solution. Today, artificial flowers can look very real and they are also very beautiful. Flower arrangements should always tie in with the colour scheme of the room. They then allow you to mix and match all shades and values you are working with, creating a wonderful combination. On top of the main flower arrangements in any room, it is often a good idea to mix in smaller doses of flowers in cans, jars, coloured bottles, tea pots, clay pots, etc., etc.

The typical locations for flowers are on the dining table, coffee table, dressers, bathroom accessories, etc., but certainly they are not exclusive to these areas. If you are using one large central arrangement in a room, do not add a second one in the same area. As an alternative, use some greenery, or indeed some smaller bunches as mentioned before.

Greenery can be used just about anywhere. Shrubs can fill a corner very well, giving life and balance to the walls. Adding an uplight on the tree will evoke mood and ambience and drama. Use uplights in the more formal areas such as living areas, dining areas and bedrooms.

Colour

If you are choosing a wall colour; paint a large section of the wall in order to view the colour in all light conditions. Even better, paint a large sample of material the same colour as the wall, and move the sample around the room to check the colour and the different ways it reacts. Even walls next to each other painted exactly the same colour can look radically different depending on the light and shadow cast on that wall. The appearance of a colour can be very different under different types of light i.e. sun-light, fluorescent light, incandescent light etc. etc. Keep samples for a number of days, in order to view how the colour looks in the light of your own rooms (fabric samples, couch cushions, carpet). When you are choosing a fabric, take as large a sample home as possible. A 2' square sample will enable you to properly view and decide on colour combinations; a small 2" square piece will not.

Painting

The key to a great paint job is in the preparation. Commence by removing as many items of furniture from the room as possible.

It may seem like a lot of trouble initially, but it will make the job go more quickly in the long run. Use cloth to cover any remaining furniture or ceiling light fitting. In addition, take down all pictures, paintings, mirrors and window treatments. Remove wall switch plates and electrical covers being extra careful with the electrics. Now it is time to inspect your surfaces. It is essential that the surface be cleaned of all dirt, grease, etc., in order for prime work to absorb properly, and to achieve smooth coat. Use a sponge to wash walls and trim. In addition, always let the surface dry properly before proceeding.

Examine the walls thoroughly for cracks, holes, nail-holes, blistered paint etc.. With the smaller holes simply fill with a few applications of a good wall filler, and using a putty knife, let it dry properly between each application. For larger holes and cracks remove the flaky material with a putty knife.

Moisten the area with water, it helps the filler adhere better. Apply filler to the hole and cover with a dry wall paper for nylon mesh, integrating it into the filler. Smooth out properly, let dry, and sand. For large and small holes, always be patient and never messy. It makes for a lot less sanding and work later on.

For the painting itself, ensure you always have plenty of light. Apply a 2" or 3" strip of masking tape around the perimeter of the ceiling, or wall (depending on which you do first, generally the ceiling is recommended). Use an adjustable extension pole and the job will go much easier. Cover a roller with paint in the paint tray and remove the excess by rolling slowly along the trays ribs. Roll approximately a 4 x 4 foot area at each given time. Be careful to apply each application evenly. Leaning to one side or other of the roller will always cause lapping. Work from

one corner of the room to the next until the ceiling or wall is complete. Always ensure that it dries thoroughly and apply a separate coat if necessary.

When finished, be sure to follow the disposable directions on all of the products you use. Don't leave half filled cans of paint lying around the house. Get rid of rags that you've been using with oil paints daily by first thoroughly soaking them in water and then disposing of them properly.

Proportion And Styling

Having the proportion and scale correct in a room or area, is just as important as getting the colours and patterns correct, when it is often something that people totally over-look! The tendency nowadays is to make the mistake of having lots of smaller items scattered about and ending up with an untidy and muddled look with no cohesion or proportion.   It is often better to have one large oversized object, but if that is impossible, then groove the smaller items together. A group of e.g. family photographs and frames on a small table looks far more impressive

than having them spread out over an entire room or area or hung on the walls individually. Additionally, smaller ornaments arranged together also look far more attractive and effective. On a couch or sofa, smaller cushions always look better when grouped together, particularly if they are made of different fabric patterns. Again, if you are able to purchase or make new cushions for a sofa, then go for the more modern look of having two or three large cushions rather than lots of small ones.

When buying pictures to hang on the wall, it is quite difficult to imagine their scale when hung, but a good rule of thumb is to buy them larger than you think you actually need, similarly, a pair of frames that are virtually the same size are so much easier to hang effectively than having an assortment of small pictures that need to be grouped together.

If you are going to decorate and furnish a brand new room, or give an existing room an overhaul, then it's always a good idea to sketch or draw a floor plan (to scale) on a sheet of graph paper. Make smaller paper templates of the furniture you intend to use, not forgetting the fireplace and other fixed items etc., and move them around until you have them looking correct. Furniture is often far darker than you think!

Always bear in mind people like to feel relaxed when sitting in a room, so try and group the furniture together to help in conversation. If left alone guests will often automatically draw their chairs closer together in order to feel comfortable. Also, when checking your scaled plan, ensure that the furniture can fit through the existing doors, something which is often overlooked!

House Designs from 1,651 up to 2,000 sq. ft.

A house is a machine for living in.
Le Corbusier (1887-1965)
Swiss-born French architect.

House C-101

Phone Lo-Call 1890 713 713 to order plans by credit card.

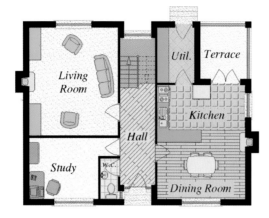

Ground floor plan

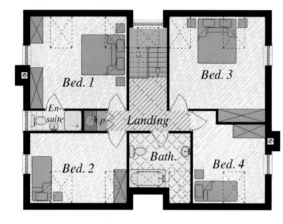

First floor plan

Hallway	4.7 x 1.9m / 15'5" x 6'2"
W.C.	1.9 x 1.0m / 6'2" x 3'3"
Study	3.4 x 3.1m / 11'2" x 10'2"
Living Room	3.4 x 4.6m / 11'2" x 15'1"
Kit / Din	5.5 x 4.6m / 18'5" x 15'1"
Utility	2.6 x 2.0m / 8'6" x 6'6"
Terrace	2.5 x 2.5m / 8'2" x 8'2"
Landing	2.4 x 1.9m / 7'10" x 6'2"
Bathroom	2.8 x 2.6m / 9'2" x 8'6"
Hot Press	0.9 x 1.0m / 2'11" x 3'3"
Bedroom 01	4.4 x 4.3m / 14'5" x 14'1"
En-Suite	2.3 x 1.0m / 7'6" x 3'3"
Bedroom 02	4.4 x 3.3m / 14'5" x 10'9"
Bedroom 03	4.4 x 4.3m / 14'5" x 14'1"
Bedroom 04	3.5 x 3.5m / 11'5" x 11'5"

AREA (excluding terrace)
172.7 sq. m. / 1,860 sq. ft.

FRONTAGE
11.6 m. / 38.1 ft.

This fantastic dormer uses all available space to its full and maximum advantage. The large roof light windows provide tremendous light to the upstairs area.

House C-102

Phone 00 353 56 71300 to order plans by credit card from outside the Republic of Ireland.

Floor plan

Hallway	3.8 x 1.8m /12'5" x 5'10"
W.C.	1.6 x 1.2m / 5'2" x 3'11"
Sitting Room	3.3 x 3.4m / 10'9" x 11'2"
Living Room	4.9 x 4.3m / 16'1" x 14'1"
Kitchen	3.9 x 3.0m / 12'9" x 9'10"
Dining	3.9 x 3.3m / 12'9" x 10'9"
Sunroom	4.2 x 3.4m / 13'9" x 11'2"
Bathroom	2.2 x 1.9m / 7'2" x 6'2"
Bedroom 01	4.1 x 4.1m / 13'5" x 13'5"
En-Suite	1.7 x 1.9m / 5'6" x 6'2"
Wardrobe	1.7 x 1.6m / 5'6" x 5'2"
Bedroom 02	3.9 x 4.0m / 12'9" x 13'1"
Bedroom 03	3.4 x 3.4m / 11'2" x 11'2"
Bedroom 04	2.9 x 2.4m / 9'6" x 7'10"

AREA
161.4 sq. m. / 1,740 sq. ft.

FRONTAGE (excluding sunroom)
16.2 m. / 53.1 ft.

Single-storey dwellings such as this with lots of character, are especially prevalent in this country in the more beautiful, restricted areas. It shows how a lower building may still have many features throughout.

House C-103

See page 104 to order this design by post.

Floor plan

Hallway	4.8 x 2.1m / 15'8" x 6'10"
Living Room	6.0 x 4.3m / 19'8" x 14'1"
Kit / Din	6.0 x 4.7m / 19'8" x 15'5"
Sitting Room	4.5 x 4.6m / 14'9" x 15'1"
Bathroom	2.5 x 2.1m / 8'2" x 6'10"
Hot Press	0.9 x 1.1m / 2'11" x 3'7"
Bedroom 01	4.2 x 4.4m / 13'9" x 14'5"
En-suite	3.6 x 1.0m / 11'9" x 3'3"
Bedroom 02	4.2 x 3.8m / 13'9" x 12'5"
Bedroom 03	3.6 x 3.8m / 11'9" x 12'5"
Bedroom 04	3.6 x 3.8m / 11'9" x 12'5"

AREA
169.4 sq. m. / 1,830 sq. ft.

FRONTAGE
18.7 m. / 61.3 ft.

The elements of this appealing house have been designed in such a way as to provide maximum accessibility throughout. The all round effect is enhanced by the simple yet effective bay window to the front.

House C-104

See page 102 for plan prices.

Floor plan

Lobby	2.2 x 2.4m / 7'2" x 7'10"
Hallway	2.8 x 2.4m / 9'2" x 7'10"
Sitting Room	5.4 x 5.4m / 17'8" x 17'8"
Living Room	4.5 x 4.6m / 14'9" x 15'1"
Kit / Din	4.8 x 3.5m / 15'8" x 11'5"
Utility	3.3 x 2.1m / 10'9" x 6'10"
Bathroom	3.3 x 2.1m / 10'9" x 6'10"
Hot Press	1.6 x 1.6m / 5'2" x 5'2"
Bedroom 01	4.3 x 3.5m / 14'1" x 11'5"
En-suite	1.8 x 1.8m / 5'10" x 5'10"
Bedroom 02	3.7 x 3.2m / 12'1" x 10'5"
En-suite	2.6 x 1.1m / 8'6" x 3'7"
Bedroom 03	3.4 x 3.2m / 11'2" x 10'5"
Bedroom 04	3.4 x 3.2m / 11'2" x 10'5"

AREA
168.5 sq. m. / 1,820 sq. ft.

FRONTAGE
20.4 m. / 66.9 ft.

This fantastic bungalow offers very well proportioned rooms together with an elegant frontage. Bear in mind that the living room can also be used as a separate dining room, where desired.

House C-105

Phone Lo-Call 1890 713 713 to order plans by credit card.

Floor plan

Hallway	4.8 x 2.8m / 15'8" x 9'2"
Kit / Din	6.1 x 4.7m / 20' x 15'5"
Playroom	3.1 x 3.0m / 10'2" x 9'10"
Utility Room	2.1 x 1.9m / 6'10" x 6'2"
W.C.	1.7 x 1.0m / 5'6" x 3'3"
Living Room	4.1 x 4.0m / 13'5" x 13'1"
Bathroom.	3.4 x 2.1m / 11'2" x 6'10"
Bedroom 01	4.5 x 3.8m / 14'9" x 12'5"
En-suite	2.2 x 1.3m / 7'2" x 4'3"
Bedroom 02	3.4 x 2.7m / 11'2" x 8'10"
Bedroom 03	3.4 x 3.6m / 11'2" x 11'9"
Bedroom 04	3.8 x 3.7m / 12'5" x 12'1"

AREA
154 sq. m. / 1657 sq. ft.

FRONTAGE
17.4 m. / 57.1 ft.

This superb family home is designed in such a way as to accommodate future expansion into the upstairs area. The dormer windows add additional prestige to the roof section.

House C-106

Phone 00 353 56 71300 to order plans by credit card from outside the Republic of Ireland.

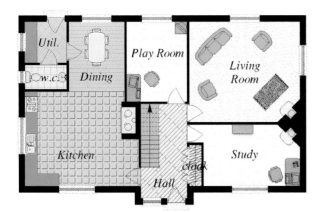

Ground floor plan

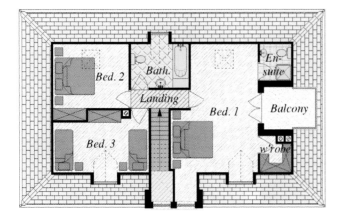

First floor plan

Hallway	4.5 x 2.4m / 14'9" x 7'10"
Kitchen	5.6 x 5.0m / 18'4" x 16'4"
Dining Room	3.0 x 2.9m / 9'10" x 9'6"
Utility	2.0 x 2.1m / 6'6" x 6'10"
W.C.	2.0 x 1.0m / 6'6" x 3'3"
Play Room	3.8 x 3.1m / 12'5" x 10'2"
Living Room	5.4 x 5.0m / 17'8" x 16'4"
Study	4.7 x 3.1m / 15'5" x 10'2"
Landing	2.8 x 2.3m / 9'2" x 7'6"
Bathroom	3.2 x 2.6m / 10'5" x 8'6"
Bedroom 01	6.2 x 3.5m / 20'4" x 11'5"
En-suite	1.7 x 1.7m / 5'6" x 5'6"
Wardrobe	1.7 x 1.7m / 5'6" x 5'6"
Balcony	2.5 x 2.2m / 8'2" x 7'2"
Bedroom 02	3.8 x 3.3m / 12'5" x 10'9"
Bedroom 03	4.8 x 3.2m / 15'8" x 10'5"

AREA
185.2 sq. m. / 1,900 sq. ft.

FRONTAGE
14.3 m. / 46.8 ft.

This design has proved to be quite versatile in the past, with the playroom and study often being used for quite different functions. The balcony off bedroom 01 can sometimes be glazed in, in order to be used right throughout the year.

House C-107

See page 104 to order this design by post.

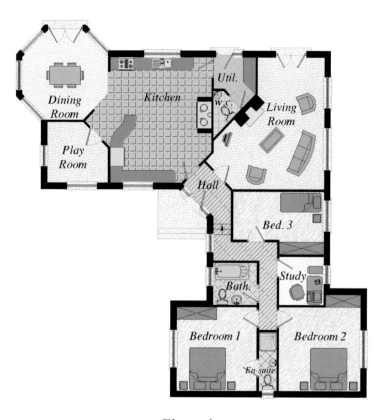

Floor plan

Hallway	2.1 x 1.5m / 6'10" x 4'11"
Kitchen	6.0 x 5.0m / 19'8" x 16'4"
Dining Room	4.2 x 4.2m / 13'9" x 13'9"
Playroom	3.0 x 2.8m / 9'10" x 9'2"
Utility	2.5 x 2.1m / 8'2" x 6'10"
W.C.	1.9 x 1.2m / 6'2" x 3'11"
Living Room	6.3 x 4.5m / 20'6" x 14'9"
Bathroom	2.2 x 2.0m / 7'2" x 6'6"
Study	2.3 x 2.2m / 7'6" x 7'2"
Bedroom 01	4.0 x 3.9m / 13'1" x 12'9"
En-Suite	2.7 x 0.9m / 8'10" x 2'11"
Bedroom 02	4.0 x 4.0m / 13'11" x 13'1"
Bedroom 03	4.5 x 2.2m / 14'9" x 7'2"

AREA
159.9 sq. m. / 1,721.14 sq. ft.

FRONTAGE (including dining)
18.8 m. / 61.6 ft.

Masterful use of space together with a stunning façade combine to create this special dwelling. The very spacious kitchen area can be completely closed off from the glazed dining area with doors, if desired.

House C-108

See page 102 for plan prices.

Floor plan

Hallway	5.2 x 3.1m / 17'1" x 10'2"
Kitchen	4.8 x 3.6m / 15'8" x 11'9"
Dining Room	6.4 x 3.5m / 20'11" x 11'5"
Utility	3.3 x 2.2m / 10'9" x 7'2"
W.C.	2.0 x 0.9m / 6'6" x 2'11"
Living Room	5.7 x 4.8m / 18'8" x 15'8"
Family Room	3.4 x 3.1m / 11'2" x 10'2"
Bathroom	3.0 x 2.4m / 9'10" x 7'10"
Hot Press	1.7 x 1.2m / 5'6" x 3'11"
Bedroom 01	4.8 x 4.1m / 15'8" x 13'5"
En-suite	2.0 x 1.8m / 6'6" x 5'10"
Bedroom 02	4.1 x 3.5m / 13'5" x 11'5"
En-suite	1.9 x 1.8m / 6'2" x 5'10"
Bedroom 03	4.1 x 2.4m / 13'5" x 7'10"
Bedroom 04	2.9 x 2.4m / 9'6" x 7'10"

AREA

171.3 sq. m. / 1,840 sq. ft.

FRONTAGE

18.7 m. / 61.3 ft.

Designed optionally in order to be constructed in separate phases. The circular bay to the site contrasts perfectly with the more conservative splayed bay window to the front and rear.

House C-109

Phone Lo-Call 1890 713 713 to order plans by credit card.

Ground floor plan

First floor plan

Hallway	2.9 x 2.7m / 9'6" x 8'10"
Living Room	4.9 x 4.9m / 16'1" x 16'1"
Kitchen	5.8 x 2.9m / 19'3" x 9'6"
Dining	2.8 x 3.0m / 9'2" x 9'10"
Utility	1.7 x 1.9m / 5'6" x 6'2"
W.C.	1.7 x 1.0m / 5'6" x 3'3"
Office	2.7 x 2.7m / 8'10" x 8'10"
Bedroom 02	4.6 x 3.6m / 15'1" x 11'9"
Landing	3.3 x 2.1m / 10'9" x 6'10"
Bathroom	2.7 x 2.7m / 8'10" x 8'10"
Bedroom 01	4.7 x 4.9m / 15'5" x 16'1"
En-Suite	1.9 x 1.8m / 6'2" x 5'10"
Balcony	3.0 x 2.3m / 9'10" x 7'6"
Bedroom 03	4.7 x 4.0m / 15'5" x 13'1"
Bedroom 04	4.6 x 3.6m / 15'1" x 11'9"

AREA (excluding balcony)
181.9 sq. m. / 1,960 sq. ft.

FRONTAGE
11.4 m. / 37.4 ft.

A house which fits just as easily into a Mediterranean landscape as it does so successfully into an Irish type setting. The downstairs bedroom is often used as a family room if required.

House C-110

See page 104 to order this design by post.

Floor plan

Hallway	5.1 x 1.7m / 16'8" x 5'6"
Kitchen/Dining	8.1 x 5.1m / 26'6" x 16'8"
Utility	2.6 x 2.0m / 8'6" x 6'6"
W.C.	2.0 x 1.2m / 6'6" x 3'11"
Living Room	4.8 x 3.9m / 15'8" x 12'9"
Hot Press	1.5 x 1.5m / 4'11" x 4'11"
Bathroom	2.9 x 2.3m / 9'6" x 7'6"
Bedroom 01	5.6 x 4.0m / 18'4" x 13'1"
En-Suite	1.9 x 1.5m / 6'2" x 4'11"
Wardrobe	1.8 x 1.5m / 5'10" x 4'11"
Bedroom 02	5.6 x 3.4m / 18'4" x 11'2"
Bedroom 03	4.0 x 2.4m / 13'1" x 7'10"
Bedroom 04	3.9 x 2.4m / 12'9" x 7'10"

AREA
164.7 sq. m. / 1,772.8 sq. ft.

FRONTAGE
18.7 m. / 61.4 ft.

Practicality is the key word for this hugely popular house design. More or less every square inch of space is used in a very sensible way, and the splayed walls to the hallway provide terrific light to the corridor area.

House C-111

Phone Lo-Call 1890 713 713 to order plans by credit card.

Ground floor plan

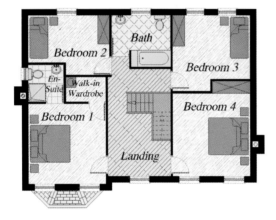

First floor plan

Hallway	4.0 x 3.2m / 13'1" x 10'5"
Study	3.9 x 3.3m / 12'9" x 10'9"
Living Room	4.8 x 3.9m / 15'8" x 12'9"
Utility	2.4 x 2.2m / 7'10" x 7'2"
W.C.	2.0 x 1.2m / 6'6" x 3'11"
Kitchen/Dining	7.9 x 3.9m / 25'9" x 12'9"
Landing	5.2 x 3.2m / 17'1" x 10'5"
Bathroom	3.0 x 2.5m / 9'10" x 8'2"
Bedroom 01	3.9 x 3.9m / 12'9" x 12'9"
En-Suite	1.8 x 1.8m / 5'10" x 5'10"
WalkInWardrobe	2.0 x 1.2m / 6'6" x 3'11"
Bedroom 02	4.1 x 2.3m / 13'5" x 7'6"
Bedroom 03	3.9 x 3.1m / 12'9" x 10'2"
Bedroom 04	4.0 x 3.9m / 13'1" x 12'9"

AREA
179.0sq. m. / 1,929.73 sq. ft.

FRONTAGE
11.8 m. / 38.7 ft.

A very deceptive two-storey. Although quite economical in size, the outside gives an impression of tremendous grandeur.

Phone 00 353 56 71300 to order plans by credit card from outside the Republic of Ireland.

Floor plan

Hallway	4.5 x 2.3m / 14'9" x 7'6"
Living Room	6.1 x 4.5m / 20' x 14'9"
Dining Room	6.1 x 3.3m / 20' x 10'9"
Sunroom	3.9 x 3.6m / 12'9" x 11'9"
Kitchen	5.0 x 4.5m / 16'4" x 14'9"
Utility	2.9 x 1.9m / 9'6" x 6'2"
W.C.	1.7 x 1.3m / 5'6" x 4'3"
Hot Press	1.3 x 1.1m / 4'3" x 3'7"
Bathroom	3.3 x 2.0m / 10'9" 6'6"
Bedroom 01	4.5 x 4.0m / 14'9" x 13'1"
En-Suite	2.2 x 1.7m / 7'2" x 5'6"
Wardrobe	2.0 x 1.6m / 6'6" x 5'2"
Bedroom 02	5.0 x 3.3m / 16'4" x 10'9"
Bedroom 03	3.8 x 3.3m / 12'5" x 10'9"
Bed 04 / Study	3.3 x 2.9m / 10'9" x 9'6"

AREA
185.5 sq. m. / 1996 sq. ft.

FRONTAGE (excluding sunroom)
19.9 m / 65.3 ft.

A range of features are included in this superb single-storey dwelling. The brick finish to the walls, offer a nice backdrop to the Georgian style windows as shown.

House C-113

See page 104 to order this design by post.

Ground floor plan

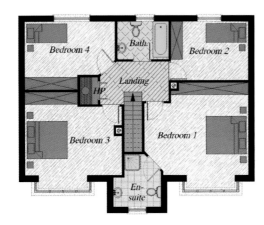

First floor plan

Hallway	6.8 x 3.1m / 22'3" x 10'2"
Sitting Room	4.8 x 4.2m / 15'8" x 13'9"
Study	3.4 x 3.1m / 11'2" x 10'2"
W.C.	2.0 x 1.2m / 6'6" x 3'11"
Utility	7.4 x 3.6m / 24'3" x 11'9"
Landing	3.4 x 2.1m / 11'2" x 6'10"
Bathroom	2.6 x 1.8m / 8'6" x 5'10"
Hot Press	1.3 x 0.9m / 4'3" x 2'11"
Bedroom 01	5.2 x 4.4m / 17'1" x 14'5"
En-Suite	2.4 x 2.4m / 7'10" x 7'10"
Bedroom 02	3.8 x 2.8m / 12'5" x 9'2"
Bedroom 03	4.8 x 4.0m / 15'8" x 13'1"
Bedroom 04	4.5 x 3.3m / 14'9" x 10'9"

AREA
176.4 sq. m. / 1,898.75 sq. ft.

FRONTAGE
11.7 m. / 38.3 ft.

A magnificent entrance hallway is the starting point and centrepiece of this spacious two-storey. Vertical emphasis to the glazing and bay windows creates a hugely impressive public frontage.

House C-114

See page 102 for plan prices.

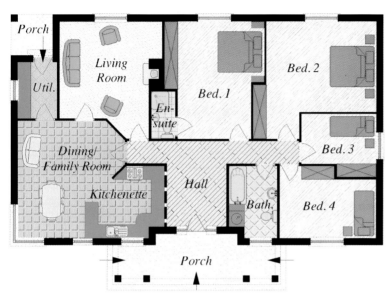

Floor plan

Hallway	3.8 x 2.7m / 12'5" x 8'9"
Dining / Family	5.2 x 4.9m / 1'1" x 16'1"
Kitchenette	3.2 x 2.4m / 10'5" x 7'10"
Utility	2.5 x 1.8m / 8'2" x 5'9"
Living Room	4.3 x 4.7m / 14'1" x 15'4"
Bathroom	3.2 x 2.2m / 10'5" x 7'2"
Bedroom 01	5.2 x 4.5m / 17'1" x 14'8"
En-suite	2.1 x 1.1m / 6'7" x 3'6"
Bedroom 02	5.0 x 4.0m / 16'4" x 13'1"
Bedroom 03	3.4 x 2.8m / 11'1" x 9'1"
Bedroom 04	4.4 x 3.2m / 14'4" x 10'5"
Rear Porch	1.6 x 1.5m / 5'2" x 4'9"

AREA(excluding porches)
150.6 sq. m. / 1,621.04 sq. ft.

FRONTAGE
16.9 m. / 55.4 ft.

This beautiful single-storey exudes a colonial feel to the exterior. An additional advantage of such houses with a high pitch is that the attic space can prove quite useful, in particular if left free of structural roof members.

House C-115

Phone Lo-Call 1890 713 713 to order plans by credit card.

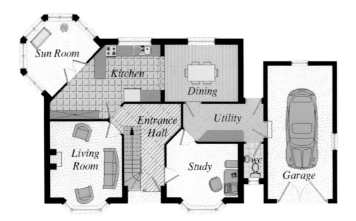

Ground floor plan

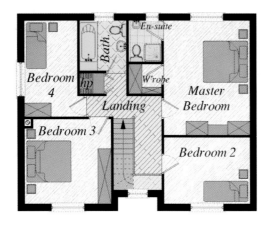

First floor plan

Hallway	4.5 x 2.2m / 14'9" x 7'2"
Living Room	4.0 x 3.9m / 13'1" x 12'9"
Kitchen	6.0 x 4.0m / 19'8" x 13'1"
Sunroom	3.7 x 3.1m / 12'1" x 10'2"
Dining Room	4.0 x 3.0m / 13'1" x 9'10"
Utility	3.2 x 2.0m / 10'5" x 6'6"
Study	3.9 x 2.8m / 12'9" x 9'2"
W.C.	2.4 x 1.1m / 7'10" x 3'7"
Garage	7.0 x 3.5m / 22'11" x 11'5"
Landing	3.4 x 0.9m / 11'2" x 2'11"
Bathroom	2.2 x 2.1m / 7'2" x 6'10"
Hot Press	1.1 x 0.9m / 3'7" x 2'11"
Master Bedroom	5.0 x 3.9m / 16'4" x 12'9"
En-Suite	1.8 x 1.5m / 5'10" x 4'11"
Wardrobe	1.5 x 1.3m / 4'11" x 4'3"
Bedroom 02	3.9 x 2.9m / 12'9" x 9'6"
Bedroom 03	3.9 x 3.7m / 12'9" x 12'1"
Bedroom 04	4.2 x 2.4m / 13'9" x 7'10"

AREA (excluding garage)
166.7 sq. m. / 1,794.34 sq. ft.
FRONTAGE (including garage)
15.9m. / 52.1 ft.

Here is a design suitable for both town and country! The character to the front is continued right through to the interior, and in particular in the entrance area.

House C-116

Phone 00 353 56 71300 to order plans by credit card from outside the Republic of Ireland.

Ground floor plan

First floor plan

Hallway	4.4 x 2.9m / 14'5" x 9'6"
Office	4.6 x 3.3m / 15'1" x 10'9"
W.C.	3.4 x 0.9m / 11'2" x 2'11"
Master Bedroom	4.4 x 4.0m / 14'5" x 13'1"
En-suite	1.9 x 1.7m / 6'2" x 5'6"
Sunroom	4.3 x 4.0m / 14'1" x 13'1"
Kitchen/Dining	4.5 x 3.1m / 14'9" x 10'2"
Living	5.8 x 4.4m / 19'3" x 14'5"
Landing	2.5 x 0.8m / 8'2" x 2'7"
Bathroom	2.7 x 2.1m / 8'10" x 6'10"
Hot Press	0.9 x 0.9m / 2'11" x 2'11"
Bedroom 02	4.4 x 3.8m / 14'5" x 12'5"
Bedroom 03	4.4 x 2.7m / 14'5" x 8'10"

AREA

170.1 sq. m. / 1,830.9 sq. ft.

FRONTAGE (including dining)

12.7m. / 41.6 ft.

This fabulous split level, both physically and mentally divides this home into separate sleeping and living areas, and obviously would greatly suit a sloping site (but not necessarily). An office area accessible from the outside is becoming more and more prevalent in our busy world.

House C-117

See page 102 for plan prices.

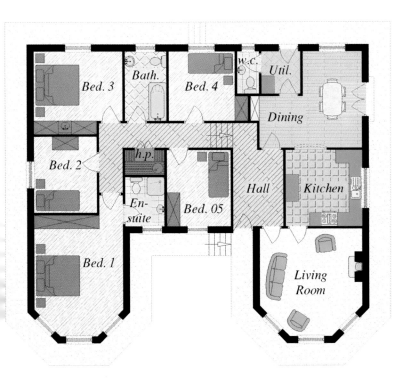

Floor plan

Hallway	4.6 x 2.3m / 15'1" x 7'6"
Kitchen	3.5 x 3.4m / 11'5" x 11'2"
Dining Room	4.3 x 2.7m / 14'1" x 8'10"
Utility	2.0 x 1.6m / 6'6" x 5'2"
W.C.	2.0 x 1.2m / 6'6" x 3'11"
Bathroom	3.1 x 1.9m / 10'2" x 6'2"
Hot Press	1.9 x 1.1m / 6'2" x 3'7"
Bedroom 01	5.4 x 4.1m / 17'8" x 13'5"
En-Suite	2.2 x 1.8m / 7'2" x 5'10"
Bedroom 02	3.4 x 2.9m / 11'2" x 9'6"
Bedroom 03	4.1 x 3.7m / 13'5" x 12'1"
Bedroom 04	3.1 x 3.0m / 10'2" x 9'10"
Bedroom 05	3.4 x 2.9m / 11'2" x 9'6"

AREA
157.4 sq. m. / 1,694.2 sq. ft.

FRONTAGE
15.6 m. / 51.2 ft.

This is a splendid single storey, which can prove to be very deceptive. The kitchen area is perfectly located and accessible both from the key dining and living room areas.

House C-118

See page 104 to order this design by post.

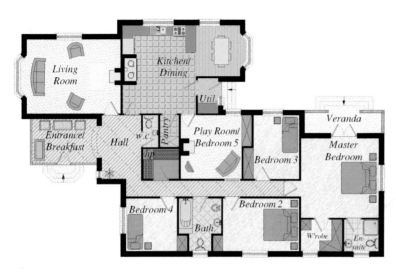

Floor plan

Entrance	3.8 x 2.6m / 12'5" x 8'6"
Hallway	3.6 x 2.3m / 11'9" x 7'6"
Living Room	5.5 x 4.2m / 18'5" x 13'9"
Kitchen	5.0 x 4.3m / 16'4" x 14'1"
Dining	2.6 x 2.9m / 11'2" x 8'6"
Utility	2.0 x 1.2m / 6'6" x 3'11"
W.C.	1.8 x 0.9m / 5'10" x 2'11"
Pantry	1.8 x 1.1m / 5'10" x 3'7"
Playroom	3.6 x 3.6m / 11'9" x 11'9"
Bathroom	3.0 x 2.5m / 9'10" x 8'2"
Hot Press	2.1 x 1.7m / 6'10" x 5'6"
Master Bedroom	4.5 x 4.5m / 14'5" x 14'5"
En-suite	2.0 x 1.8m / 6'6" x 5'10"
Wardrobe	2.4 x 1.8m / 7'10" x 510"
Veranda	4.5 x 1.1m / 14'9" x 3'7"
Bedroom 02	4.5 x 3.0m / 14'9" x 9'10"
Bedroom 03	3.0 x 3.0m / 9'10" x 9'10"
Bedroom 04	3.6 x 2.7m / 11'9" x 8'10"

AREA (excluding veranda)
168.8 sq. m. / 1816.9 sq. ft.
FRONTAGE
21.2m. / 69 ft.

A wealth of features and ideas are shown in this stunning bungalow design. Bear in mind that items such as the glazed area to the entrance and timber area to the veranda can easily be constructed at a later date where the initial budget does not cover the overall cost.

CARLOW

KIWI CONSTRUCTION LTD.
Graignamanagh,
Co. Kilkenny
Tel/Fax: 0503-24588. Mobile: 087-2631164
Also operating in Counties Kilkenny and Wexford.

EDWARD NOLAN (OLD LEIGHLIN) LTD.
Old Leighlin,
Co. Carlow
Tel/Fax: 0503-22255

FITZPATRICK CONSTRUCTIONS (CARLOW) LTD.
The Old Schoolhouse,
Killabbaun,
Ballylinan,
Athy,
Co. Kildare
Tel: 0503-45533/086-8169345 Fax: 0503-45523
Operating throughout the south-east

GALWAY

THOMAS MCHUGH
Kilcloghans, Tuam
Co. Galway
Tel/Fax: 093-28486

KERRY

JIMMY O'CONNELL CONSTRUCTION (HOMEBOND)
18. Main Street,
Kenmare,
Co. Kerry
Tel: 064-41354 / 087-2486410. Fax: 064-41354
E-mail: 2brnot2b@eircom.net

KILKENNY

DOMINIC DELANEY BUILDING CONTRACTOR
Knockeenbaun,
Kilmanagh,
Co. Kilkenny
Tel/Fax: 056-69170. Mobile: 086-2535793

PATSY MURPHY BUILDING CONTRACTOR
The Square, Ballyragget, Co. Kilkenny
Tel./Fax: 056-33649 Mobile: 086-2461534
Also operating in Co. Laois

ASHGROVE CONSTRUCTION KILKENNY LTD.
Templemartin,
Clara,
Co. Kilkenny
Tel/Fax: 056-52615. Mobile: 087-2331717

CHRISTY COMERFORD BUILDING CONTRACTOR
Sycamore Drive,
Ardnore,
Kilkenny
Tel: 086-8169558

LIMERICK

TIM O'RIORDAN CONTRACTORS (HOMEBOND)
Farnane,
Munroe,
Co. Limerick
Tel/Fax: 061-386170 / 087-2654166

CONOR KELLY BUILDING
St. James, Newtown,
Clarina, Co. Limerick
Tel/Fax: 061-353030. Mobile: 086-8122276

GERARD KINEVANE BUILDING & CARPENTRYCONTRACTOR(HOMEBOND)
Tuogh, Adare,
Co. Limerick
Tel/Fax: 061-395193 / 086-2755584

MEATH

DAMIAN CAMPBELL BUILDING CONTRACTOR (HOMEBOND)
Tel: 041-9826565 / 086-2603303
Operating in Louth and Meath

OFFALY

KEVIN O'REILLY
Knockballyboy,
Daingean,
Co. Offaly
Tel: 0506-53721 / 086-8131081

SLIGO

SEAN KILGANNON CONSTRUCTION
Ballyglass,
Templeboy
Co. Sligo
Tel/Fax: 096-47209 / 086-2617193

TIPPERARY

ROSKEEN CONSTRUCTION LTD.
Nodstown,
Boherlahan,
Cashel,
Co. Tipperary
Tel/Fax: 0504 - 41256 / 087 - 2531871
Also operating throughout Limerick, Kilkenny, Cork, Tipperary/Clare border.

WEXFORD

JODAN DEVELOPMENTS LTD.
Aughclare,
New Ross,
Co. Wexford
Tel/Fax: 051-388770
E-mail: jodandan@indigofree.ie
Also operating throughout the south-east

Are you building or extending your present home?

Then consider Ireland's Number One Underfloor Heating System

Further information from:

**Heatlink Ireland,
Cappincur,
Tullamore,
Co .Offaly.**

Tel: (0506) 24062 / 24118
Fax: (0506) 24063
Freephone: 1800 311 338
Email: hlinkirl@aol.com
Web: www.Heat.Link.com
http://www.Heatlink.com

Also at:

**Heatlink Ireland,
Thomastown,
Co. Kilkenny.**

Tel: (056) 54964
Fax: (056) 54961

Your Heat link to Warm Feet

Imagine standing barefoot outdoors on a crisp, sunny autumn day The path you are standing on has absorbed the day's heat and now your feet have the pleasure of enjoying the delicious warmth held within.

Well this sensation could be brought to your home by HeatLink Underfloor Heating Systems. Your comfort is paramount to Heatlink; their feet have felt the cold lino of conventional heating systems and are standing on warmed flooring waiting to talk to you.

They will list the reasons why underfloor heating is the best solution to heating your home. Starting with comfort, warm feet equal sunny disposition!, followed by draught elimination. Some systems draw cold air in; with HeatLink; warm air rises sedately and doesn't have that great desire of heat generated by other systems to escape. Another good reason to choose Heatlink is the total lack of radiators, which really remind you, by their sheer presence, that, for the majority of the year we live in a cold grey climate with only glimpses of the salad days of summer.

With this system, stepping into your home on a cold winter's evening you will feel like stepping into sandals rather than slippers.

Other Reasons to choose HeatLink

With forced-air and radiator heating there are areas of the home that never seem to feel warm, the heat never reaches them and during the winter months these areas become unused, families retreat to the living room to eat meals because no matter how long the radiator is on or however high the setting, the room remains uncomfortably cold. HeatLink ensures even heating throughout the entire house, touching all surfaces. The system also allows great flexibility when it comes to furniture arrangement, too.

How many times have you moved furniture around to suit the position of the radiator. During the summer months, furniture can be placed where you would ideally like to leave it, but as soon as the leaves turn brown in autumn there is the sudden and almost primitive need to huddle into areas of warmth - radiators, all ideals fly out the window and furniture is pulled up to the source of heat and remains there for the duration of the winter...

Experience Barefoot Comfort

With forced-air or radiator led systems, there is always the need to both conceal the radiator with heat blocking furniture or spend money trying to make it appear different, for instance by using a radiator cover. Another thing we are prone to do is pile damp, steaming clothes on all available radiators and have streams of condensation running down the windows. HeatLink eliminates all that and frees your home from the tyranny of becoming a giant winter airing cupboard!

Another thing about radiators now that I've started is painting the blessed things and the wall behind. This may be a small problem to some people, but to others like myself it has become a battle of wills. Many times I have been tempted to pull the radiator off the wall in my attempts to roller that wall in the new colour of the season. And you cannot just leave the radiators virginal white, no the urge to make them blend in with their surroundings is too great and from the moment you put a paint laden brush near them you have become a slave to the art of radiator painting. For me this is one extremely good reason to go for an underfloor system, which will allow you to glide around each room with a large rollerbrush with no need to dart venomous glances at the thing that will cause you many hours of consternation.

How It Works...

At its most basic, underfloor heating involves heating a structure by pumping warm water through specially designed tubing laid under or within the floor. The heat in these tubes radiates to the surface and rises evenly throughout the room above. The surface itself stays comfortably warm to the touch. This tremendously efficient heat transfer results in even and consistent heating.

Warm air rises, of course and collects near the ceiling. In a home heated by convection, ceilings are always warmer than floors. With underfloor heating the opposite is true. The floor is warm and so is the air up to the height sensed by the occupants. Thus, people within the space feel much more comfortable at lower temperature settings because the heat is coming from the floor. HeatLink PEX tubing which delivers the heat is laid on the subfloor and covered with a flowable lightweight concrete. It can also be installed in the lower level concrete floor or underneath the joist space, which is called a 'dry' or 'staple-up' installation.

The system allows any floor surface to be placed above it, including carpeting, ceramic tile, vinyl flooring and wood.

Heating with a sunny disposition

Underfloor heating systems are powered by a boiler or a special water heater; therefore, no furnace is needed. Often, the floor heating system can be combined with high velocity air conditioning and a potable hot water delivery system for cooking, bathing and laundry Many homes these days do not follow the conventional architectural theme, Irish people have become more creative, more aware of design and architecture and when building a home are insisting on their own input into the design.

Buildings with higher ceilings are not suited to the conventional systems as larger open areas require ceiling fans to blow air up or down, depending on the time of year. But with a underfloor system, warm air is already right where it is needed. Think of it this way, when you are sitting down to watch TV if you have a forced air or radiator system, often you must turn the heat up to be comfortable, with radiant heat you can actually turn it down because you are closer to the floor; which is the source of the heat.

Feeling the Heat

With this system the surface area of the floor is designed to be no higher than 88°F/31°C, so it is always comfortable to walk on. HeatLink operates at the lowest possible water temperature to heat the structure. This level provides the most efficient transfer of energy. There are no wide temperature variations that you experience with forced air or radiator systems. It is also very quiet!! as there are no fans pushing heat around, no clunk, clunk of radiators

expanding and no hot and cold spots that you collide with on your journeys around your home, all you have is quiet, comfortable warmth.

Energy efficiency is one of the system's strong points because the system delivers heat where it's needed, with little waste. A thermostat can be put in every room of the house and little used rooms can be set to low heat settings, so the room is warmed but not heated to the same level as the most frequently used rooms, allowing you control your heating which will, in consequence, save you money.

HeatLink provide the latest technology in controls which gives you the customer the ultimate in an automated controlled heating system at the customers own desired temperatures.

The package

Heatlink have devised special software in order to help clients to visualise what will be happening in their home before, during and after installation of the system, allowing the client to view the plans and modify the placement of the tubing to suit their particular needs. Once the nitty gritty planning stage is out of the way installation of the system itself is simple and usually carried out by a plumbing and heating contractor. HeatLink have devised installation tools that make it even easier to install, which HeatLink believes makes them the first choice for contractors ... if the contractors needs any assistance HeatLink will help. Alternatively HeatLink can provide a full installation service carried out by their own installation engineers. The actually running costs of the system are low which in turn reduces the amount you spend on heating your home annually.

The HeatLink underfloor heating system carries with it a 25 year warranty on all tubing which incorporates a l 0 year consequential damage warranty A HeatLink system delivers the ultimate in comfort - plus it's energy efficient, safe and very reliable.

Heatlink offer the solution to all heating problems literally at your feet.

Our Customers walk all over us!

Section D

House Designs from 2,001 up to 2,500 sq. ft.

Not many sounds in life, and I include all urban and all rural sounds, exceed in interest a knock at the door.
Charles Lamb (1775 - 1834). English essayist and critic.

House D-101

See page 104 to order this design by post.

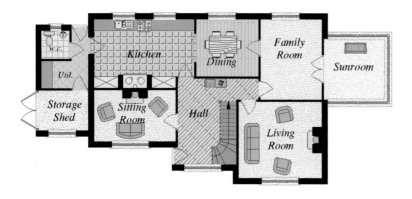

Ground floor plan

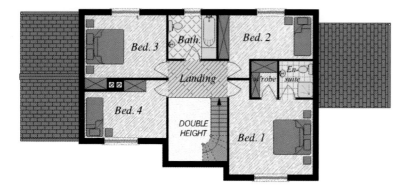

First floor plan

Hallway	4.4 x 2.4m / 14'5" x 7'10"
Sitting Room	4.3 x 2.8m / 14'1" x 9'2"
Kitchen	5.3 x 3.7m / 17'4" x 12'1"
Utility	1.7 x 1.7m / 5'6" x 5'6"
Storage Shed	3.4 x 2.7m / 11'2" x 8'10"
W.C.	1.7 x 1.0m / 5'6" x 3'3"
Dining Room	3.3 x 2.9m / 10'9" x 9'6"
Family Room	4.1 x 3.4m / 13'5" x 11'2"
Sunroom	3.2 x 3.3m / 10'5" x 10'9"
Living Room	4.4 x 4.1m / 14'5" x 13'5"
Landing	3.1 x 2.0m / 10'2" x 6'6"
Bathroom	2.5 x 2.4m / 8'2" x 7'10"
Bedroom 01	4.4 x 4.1m / 14'5" x 13'5"
En-suite	1.8 x 1.9m / 5'10" x 6'2"
Wardrobe	1.8 x 1.5m / 5'10" x 4'11"
Bedroom 02	5.0 x 2.4m / 16'4" x 7'10"
Bedroom 03	4.3 x 3.4m / 14'1" x 11'2"
Bedroom 04	4.3 x 3.2m / 14'1" x 10'5"

AREA (including shed)
208.0 sq. m. / 2,240 sq. ft.
FRONTAGE (excluding sunroom)
15.8 m. / 51.9 ft.

This fabulous family home offers a large variety of rooms with different usages. The cathedral type ceiling over the entrance hallway allows lots of light to both floors and provides a great feeling of spaciousness.

See page 102 for plan prices.

Ground floor plan

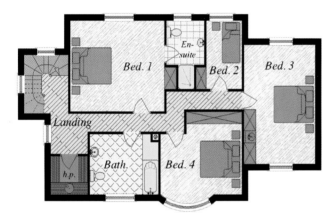

First floor plan

Hallway	2.8 x 2.0m / 9'2" x 6'6"
Dining Room	4.4 x 3.6m / 14'5" x 11'9"
Sitting Room	4.0 x 3.9m / 13'1" x 12'9"
Kitchen	4.4 x 3.0m / 14'5" x 9'10"
Utility	3.8 x 2.2m / 12'5" x 7'2"
Study	3.4 x 3.1m / 11'2" x 10'2"
W.C.	1.8 x 1.1m / 5'10" x 3'7"
Garage	5.8 x 3.6m / 19'3" x 11'9"
Landing	1.9 x 2.0m / 6'2" x 6'6"
Bathroom	3.4 x 3.1m / 11'2" x 10'2"
Hot Press	1.8 x 2.0m / 5'10" x 6'6"
Bedroom 01	4.7 x 4.6m / 15'5" x 15'1"
En-Suite	2.1 x 2.0m / 6'10" x 6'6"
Bedroom 02	3.3 x 1.9m / 10'9" x 6'2"
Bedroom 03	5.8 x 3.8m / 19'3" x 12'5"
Bedroom 04	4.0 x 4.1m / 13'1" x 13'5"

AREA (excluding garage)
194.7 sq. m. / 2,095 sq. ft.

FRONTAGE
14.1 m. / 46.2 ft.

Based on a Germanic style. The position of the stairs in particular is an unusual and popular feature of this type of dwelling.

House D-103

Phone Lo-Call 1890 713 713 to order plans by credit card.

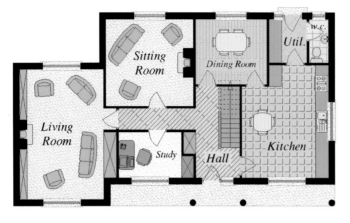

Ground floor plan

First floor plan

Hallway	4.1 x 1.2m / 13'5" x 3'11"
Study	2.9 x 2.2m / 9'6" x 7'2"
Living Room	5.9 x 4.1m / 19'4" x 13'5"
Sitting Room	4.1 x 4.1m / 13'5" x 13'5"
Kitchen	5.1 x 4.2m / 16'8" x 13'9"
Dining	3.3 x 3.1m / 10'9" x 10'2"
Utility	1.9 x 1.9m / 6'2" x 6'2"
W.C.	1.9 x 1.0m / 6'2" x 3'3"
Landing	4.7 x 1.0m / 15'5" x 3'3"
Bathroom	2.4 x 2.5m / 7'10" x 8'2"
Hot Press	1.2 x 1.1m / 3'11" x 3'7"
Bedroom 01	4.1 x 3.9m / 13'5" x 12'9"
En-Suite	2.0 x 2.0 m / 6'6" x 6'6"
Bedroom 02	4.0 x 3.9m / 13'1" x 12'9"
En-suite	2.2 x 1.4m / 7'2" x 4'7"
Bedroom 03	4.0 x 2.2m / 13'1" x 7'2"
Bedroom 04	4.5 x 3.5m / 14'9" x 11'5"

AREA
193.2 sq. m. / 2,080 sq. ft.
FRONTAGE
15.3 m. / 50.1 ft.

Based on an indigenous Irish farmhouse, but with some added features, this two-storey has just about everything! Very often used partly as a Bed & Breakfast / Guesthouse.

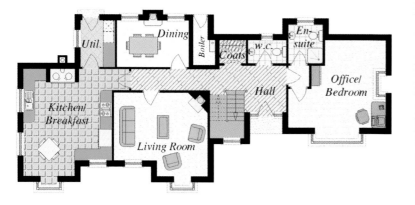

Ground floor plan

First floor plan

Hallway	3.6 x 2.3m / 11'9" x 7'6"
Living Room	4.2 x 2.8m / 13'9" x 9'2"
Kitchen	5.4 x 4.7m / 17'8" x 15'5"
Utility Room	2.3 x 2.1m / 7'6" x 6'10"
Dining Room	3.7 x 2.5m / 12'1" x 8'2"
Boiler	2.8 x 1.1m / 9'2" x 3'7"
W.C.	1.3 x 1.3m / 4'3" x 4'3"
Office	5.0 x 4.6m / 16'4" x 15'1"
En-suite	1.7 x 1.9m / 5'6" x 6'2"
Landing	5.7 x 1.2m / 18'8" x 3'11"
Bathroom	2.8 x 2.5m / 9'2" x 8'2"
Hot Press	1.5 x 1.6m / 4'11" x 5'2"
Bedroom 01	5.0 x 4.6m / 16'4" x 15'1"
En-suite	2.0 x 1.5m / 6'6" x 4'11"
Wardrobe	1.1 x 0.2m / 3'7" x 7"
Bedroom 02	4.7 x 2.8m / 15'5" x 9'2"
Bedroom 03	5.9 x 3.9m / 19'4" x 12'9"
Bedroom 04	3.8 x 2.5m / 12'5" x 8'2"

AREA
195.2 sq. m. / 2,100 sq. ft.
FRONTAGE
17.1 m. / 56.1 ft.

This amazing dwelling combines a multitude of features with highly accessible and spacious rooms. The downstairs office with en-suite would ideally serve as a bedroom for a retired couple.

House D-105

See page 104 to order this design by post.

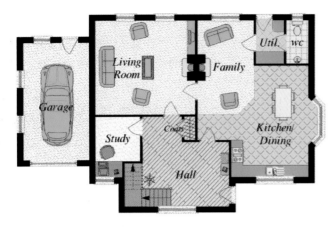

Ground floor plan

First floor plan

Hallway	5.4 x 3.4m / 17'4" x 11'2"
Study	3.0 x 2.5m / 9'10" x 8'2"
Living Room	5.2 x 4.9m / 17'1" x 16'1"
Family Room	6.0 x 3.1m / 19'8" x 10'2"
Kit / Din	5.6 x 4.2m / 18'4" x 13'9"
Utility	2.7 x 2.3m / 8'10" x 7'6"
Garage	5.9 x 3.6m / 19'4" x 11'9"
Landing	2.5 x 2.4m / 8'2" x 7'10"
Bathroom	3.7 x 3.4m / 12'1" x 11'2"
Hot Press	2.2 x 1.6m / 7'2" x 5'2"
Bedroom 01	5.4 x 4.2m / 17'8" x 13'9"
En-suite	2.3 x 2.1m / 7'6" x 6'10"
Bedroom 02	4.6 x 3.6m / 15'1" x 11'9"
En-suite	2.3 x 2.1m / 7'6" x 6'10"
Bedroom 03	4.6 x 3.6m / 15'1" x 11'9"
Bedroom 04	5.9 x 3.8m / 19'4" x 12'5"

AREA (excluding garage)
220.6 sq. m. / 2,375 sq. ft.

FRONTAGE
15.7 m. / 51.5 ft.

This house offers fantastic light and airiness, especially due to its open plan characteristics. The study can extend further into the hallway if desired.

See page 102 for plan prices.

Ground floor plan

Hallway	4.0 x 3.9m / 13'1" x 12'9"
Living Room	5.1 x 3.7m / 16'8" x 12'1"
Family Room	5.1 x 4.1m / 16'8" x 13'5"
Kitchen	3.9 x 3.7m / 12'9" x 12'1"
Dining Room	4.8 x 3.2m / 15'8" x 10'5"
Garage	5.9 x 3.6m / 19'4" x 11'9"
W.C.	2.1 x 1.2m / 6'10" x 3'11"
Store	1.1 x 1.2m / 3'7" x 3'11"
Bathroom	5.6 x 4.1m / 18'4" x 13'5"
Hot Press	0.8 x 1.0m / 2'7" x 3'3"
Bedroom 01	4.4 x 4.5m / 14'5" x 14'9"
En-suite	2.2 x 2.0m / 7'2" x 6'6"
Bedroom 02	5.6 x 3.1m / 18'4" x 10'2"
En-suite	2.2 x 1.6m / 7'2" x 5'2"
Bedroom 03	4.4 x 4.2m / 14'5" x 13'9"
Bedroom 04	4.0 x 3.4m / 13'1" x 11'2"

AREA (excluding garage)
191 sq. m. / 2,055 sq. ft.

FRONTAGE
17.7 m. / 58.1 ft.

This is a very accessible bungalow and has proved to be very popular. The extra wide hallway also allows for future expansion into the large and spacious attic space.

Phone Lo-Call 1890 713 713 to order plans by credit card.

Ground floor plan

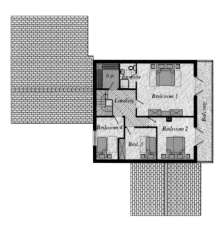

First floor plan

Hallway	6.6 x 4.0m / 21'7" x 13'1"
Bathroom	2.9 x 2.4m / 9'6" x 7'10"
Sauna	2.4 x 1.8m / 7'10" x 5'10"
Utility	2.4 x 2.2m / 7'10" x 7'2"
Kitchen/Dining	5.0 x 5.0m / 16'4" x 16'4"
Living Room	5.5 x 5.5m / 18'5" x 18'5"
Sunroom	5.5 x 3.0m / 18'5" x 9'10"
Store	2.3 x 2.5m / 7'6" x 8'2"
Workshop	5.0 x 5.0m / 16'4" x 16'4"
Landing	2.5 x 2.3m / 8'2" x 7'6"
Hot Press	2.4 x 2.2m / 7'10" x 7'2"
Bedroom 01	5.6 x 5.0m / 18'4" x 16'4"
En-suite	2.4 x 1.6m / 7'10" x 5'2"
Balcony	9.4 x 1.5m / 30'8" x 4'11"
Bedroom 02	4.0 x 3.6m / 13'1" x 11'9"
Bedroom 03	3.7 x 3.0m / 12'1" x 9'10"
Bedroom 04	4.0 x 2.7 m / 13'1" x 8'10"

AREA (excluding balcony and workshop)
205.6 sq. m. / 2,213 sq. ft.

FRONTAGE (excluding dining)
17.9m. / 58.7 ft.

This is first and foremost a very practical dwelling in layout, combined with a beautiful American style frontage. Always check with your local planning authority regarding permission for a workshop, and in particular where it is to be used for commercial purposes.

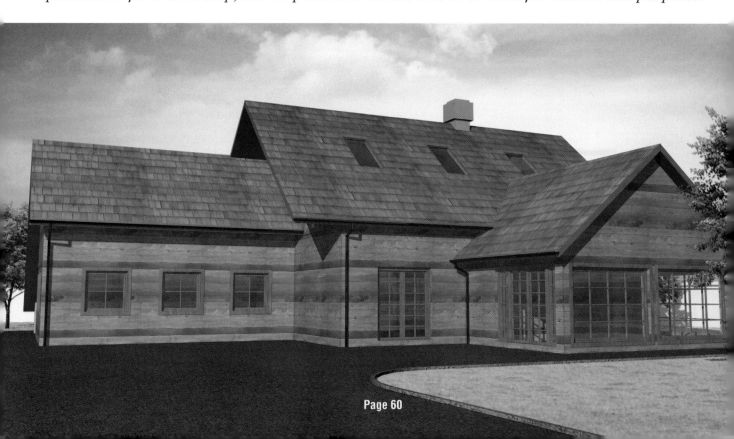

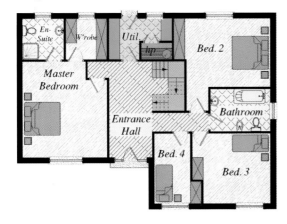

Ground floor plan

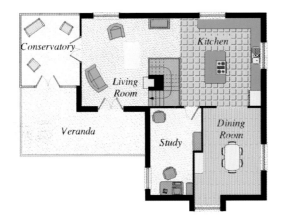

First floor plan

Hallway	5.1 x 2.5m / 16'8" x 8'2"
Utility Room	3.4 x 2.3m / 11'2" x 7'6"
Hot Press	1.6 x 1.0m / 5'2" x 3'3"
Bathroom.	3.2 x 2.4m / 10'5" x 7'10"
Bedroom 01	5.1 x 4.8m / 16'8" x 15'8"
En-suite	2.2 x 2.3m / 7'2" x 7'6"
Wardrobe	2.3 x 2.3m / 7'6" x 7'6"
Bedroom 02	4.6 x 3.8m / 15'1" x 12'5"
Bedroom 03	4.2 x 3.9m / 13'9" x 12'9"
Bedroom 04	3.7 x 2.1m / 12'1" x 6'10"
Liv / Kit	10.3 x 5.1m / 33'9" x 16'8"
Dining	4.9 x 3.5m / 16'1" x 11'5"
Study	4.9 x 3.1m / 16'1" x 10'2"
Conservatory	3.9 x 3.6m / 12'9" x 11'9"
Veranda	7.1 x 2.5m / 23'3" x 8'2"

AREA (excluding veranda)
215.8 sq. m. / 2,320 sq. ft.

FRONTAGE
14.3 m. / 46.9 ft.

What a pleasant departure from standard Irish design, with this beautiful, mid-continental style two-storey. Be sure to utilise the balcony side of the dwelling, by having it on the sunny side of your site.

A Room with a View

Add space, value, comfort and class to your home with a sun lounge
– *Made easy with a Keystone Lintel*

A sun lounge offers:
- ***Much better heat retention in winter***
- ***Protection from the blazing summer sun***
- ***Noise reduction such as that associated with rainfall on a glass roof***

The construction of a Sun Lounge has been simplified by the introduction of the **Keystone Sun Lounge Lintel**. This is a one piece unit which allows architects to design the Sun Lounge to suit the property, and will keep costs at a sensible level. The Keystone Sun Lounge Lintel is manufactured and delivered ready for erection.

Its as easy as...

Sun Lounge Lintel

See page 102 for plan prices.

Ground floor plan

First floor plan

Porch	2.1 x 1.3m / 6'10" x 4'3"
Hallway	6.3 x 2.1m / 20'6" x 6'10"
Living Room	5.3 x 4.1m / 17'4" x 13'5"
Kitchen/Dining	6.3 x 5.8m / 20'6" x 19'3"
Sunroom	3.6 x 4.0m / 11'9" x 13'1"
Utility	2.2 x 1.7m / 7'2" x 5'6"
W.C.	2.2 x 1.2m / 7'2" x 3'11"
Study	3.5 x 3.0m / 11'5" x 9'10"
Garage	5.9 x 3.0m / 19'4" x 9'10"
Landing	4.2 x 1.0m / 13'9" x 3'3"
Bathroom	3.1 x 3.1m / 10'2" x 10'2"
Hot Press	1.9 x 1.7m / 6'2" x 5'6"
Bedroom 01	4.7 x 4.2m / 15'5" x 13'9"
En-Suite	3.1 x 2.0m / 10'2" x 6'6"
Bedroom 02	4.5 x 3.0m / 14'9" x 9'10"
Bedroom 03	3.1 x 3.0m / 10'2" x 9'10"
Bedroom 04	3.1 x 3.1m / 10'2" x 10'2"

AREA (excluding garage)
202.6 sq. m. / 2,180.8 sq. ft.

FRONTAGE (excluding sunroom)
10.0 m. / 32.8 ft.

Always bear in mind with a concept shown such as this, that the sunroom can easily be omitted if necessary. It can therefore prove effective on a restrictive site.

House D-110

Phone Lo-Call 1890 713 713 to order plans by credit card.

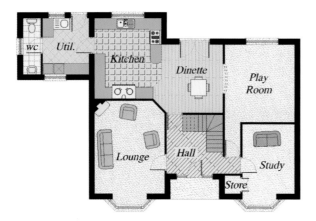

Ground floor plan

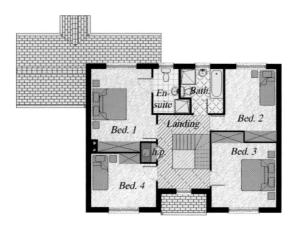

First floor plan

Hallway	3.1 x 3.1m / 10'2" x 10'2"
Lounge	5.0 x 3.9m / 16'4" x 12'9"
Kitchen	4.3 x 3.7m / 14'1" x 12'1"
Utility	3.0 x 2.6m / 9'10" x 8'6"
W.C.	3.0 x 1.0m / 9'10" x 3'3"
Dinette	3.7 x 3.5m / 12'1" x 11'5"
Playroom	4.2 x 3.9m / 13'9" x 12'9"
Study	3.7 x 2.9m / 12'1" x 9'6"
Store	1.0 x 0.9m / 3'3" x 2'11"
Landing	4.3 x 3.1m / 14'1" x 10'2"
Bathroom	2.6 x 2.6m / 8'6" x 8'6"
Hot Press	1.1 x 0.9m / 3'7" x 2'11"
Bedroom 01	4.8 x 3.6m / 15'8" x 11'9"
En-Suite	2.6 x 1.6m / 8'6" x 5'2"
Bedroom 02	4.2 x 3.1m / 13'9" x 10'2"
Bedroom 03	4.4 x 3.9m / 14'5" x 12'9"
Bedroom 04	3.9 x 3.1m / 12'9" x 10'2"

AREA
187.0sq. m. / 2,012.84 sq. ft.

FRONTAGE (excluding utility and w.c.)
11.7 m. / 38.4 ft.

This family home was essentially designed with the dinette as a centre piece, and all elements radiating from that point.

Ground floor plan

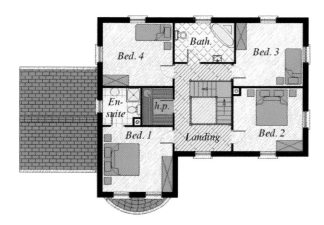

First floor plan

Hallway	3.9 x 3.3m / 12'9" x 10'9"
Living Room	4.1 x 4.0m / 13'5" x 13'1"
Dining Room	4.6 x 4.0m / 15'1" x 13'1"
Kit. / Breakfast	5.3 x 5.0m / 17'4" x 16'4"
Utility	3.2 x 2.2m / 10'5" x 7'2"
W.C.	2.0 x 1.2m / 6'6" x 3'11"
Boiler	2.2 x 0.9m / 7'2" x 2'11"
Sitting Room	4.9 x 4.0m / 16'1" x 13'1"
Landing	4.9 x 3.3m / 16'1" x 10'9"
Bathroom	3.5 x 2.2m / 11'5" x 7'2"
Hot Press	2.1 x 1.8m / 6'10" x 5'10"
Bedroom 01	4.0 x 3.7m / 13'1" x 12'1"
En-Suite	2.2 x 2.1m / 7'2" x 6'10"
Bedroom 02	4.0 x 3.6m / 13'1" x 11'9"
Bedroom 03	4.0 x 3.6m / 13'1" x 11'9"
Bedroom 04	4.0 x 3.6m / 13'1" x 11'9"

AREA
203.9 sq. m. / 2,194.7 sq. ft.

FRONTAGE (including dining)
16.3 m. / 53.5 ft.

The treatment finishes to this house combine the use of stone and brick especially well. All the rooms to the top floor are good size, double bedrooms.

House D-112

See page 102 for plan prices.

Ground floor plan

First floor plan

Hallway	3.2 x 1.9m / 10'5" x 6'2"
Lounge	6.0 x 4.8m / 19'8" x 15'8"
Boiler	1.8 x 1.5m / 18'4" x 13'5"
W.C.	1.8 x 1.5m / 5'10" x 4'11"
Utility	2.6 x 1.8m / 8'6" x 5'10"
Kitchen/Dining	5.8 x 3.9m / 19'3" x 12'9"
Sun Room	3.6 x 3.2m / 11'9" x 10'5"
Living Room	4.8 x 3.9m / 15'8" x 12'9"
Landing	3.0 x 1.8m / 9'10" x 5'10"
Bathroom	3.0 x 2.0m / 9'10" x 6'6"
Hot Press	2.0 x 1.6m / 6'6" x 5'2"
Bedroom 01	5.8 x 3.7m / 19'3" x 12'1"
En-suite	2.0 x 2.0m / 6'6" x 6'6"
Bedroom 02	5.8 x 3.9m / 19'3" x 12'9"
Bedroom 03	4.8 x 4.5m / 15'8" x 14'9"

AREA
195.3 sq. m. / 2,102.2 sq. ft.

FRONTAGE (excluding sunroom)
12.3 m. / 40.4 ft.

This type of house has become a very popular element in the Irish landscape, and you can see why! Here we see a very good example of how bay windows can add tremendously to the aesthetics of a nice dwelling.

See page 104 to order this design by post.

Ground floor plan

First floor plan

Hallway	3.7 x 3.7m / 12'1" x 12'1"
Sitting Room	5.4 x 4.1m / 17'8" x 13'5"
Dining Room	4.1 x 3.4m / 13'5" x 11'2"
Kitchen	5.1 x 4.1m / 16'8" x 13'5"
Utility	2.5 x 1.8m / 8'2" x 5'10"
W.C.	1.5 x 1.5m / 4'11" x 4'11"
Living Room	4.3 x 3.2m / 14'1" x 10'5"
Landing	5.1 x 3.7m / 16'8" x 12'1"
Bathroom	2.8 x 2.7m / 9'2" x10'5"
Hot Press	1.9 x 1.6m / 6'2" x 5'2"
Bedroom 01	4.1 x 4.0m / 13'5" x 13'1"
En-Suite	2.0 x 1.6m / 6'6" x 5'2"
Bedroom 02	4.4 x 3.8m / 14'5" x 12'5"
Bedroom 03	3.8 x 3.4m / 12'5" x 11'2"
Bedroom 04	4.4 x 3.2m / 14'5" x 10'5"

AREA
188.4 sq. m. / 2,027.9 sq. ft.

FRONTAGE
11.7m. / 38.3 ft.

This very elegant two-storey shows how a straightforward and popular concept can be very enhanced with the use of brick. This design concept borrows heavily from the popular "executive" style home.

House D-114

Phone Lo-Call 1890 713 713 to order plans by credit card.

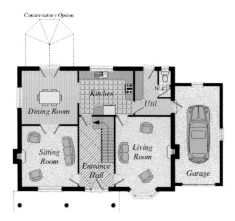

Ground floor plan

First floor plan

Hallway	5.1 x 2.6m / 16'8" x 8'6"
Sitting Room	4.4 x 4.2m / 14'5" x 13'9"
Dining	4.2 x 3.9m / 13'9" x 12'9"
Kitchen	3.8 x 3.2m / 12'5" x 10'5"
Utility	3.2 x 1.7m / 10'5" x 3'3"
W.C.	2.0 x 1.2m / 6'6" x 3'11"
Living Room	5.1 x 4.2 m / 16'8" x 13'9"
Garage	7.0 x 3.4m / 22'11" x 11'2"
Landing	4.1 x 0.9m / 13'5" x 2'11"
Bathroom	2.9 x 2.2m / 9'6" x 7'2"
Hot Press	1.1 x 1.0m / 3'7" x 3'3"
Bedroom 01	5.6 x 4.2m / 18'4" x 13'9"
En-suite	3.3 x 2.3m / 10'9" x 7'6"
Wardrobe	3.3 x 2.3m / 10'9" x 7'6"
Bedroom 02	4.2 x 2.7m / 13'9" x 8'10"
Bedroom 03	3.9 x 3.8m / 12'9" x 12'5"
Bedroom 04	4.5 x 3.3m / 14'9" x 10'9"
Bedroom 05	4.1 x 2.5m / 13'5" x 8'2"

AREA

206.2sq. m. / 2,219.5 sq. ft.

FRONTAGE

15.4 m. / 50.5 ft.

This superb two-storey has all the elements of a classic Tudor style family home. The extensive area above the garage is utilised fully.

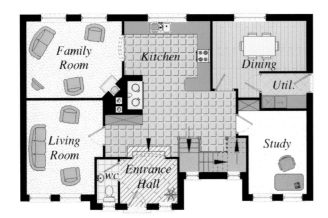

Ground floor plan

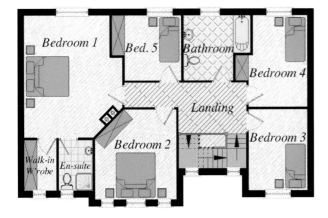

First floor plan

Hallway	2.7 x 2.2m / 8'10" x 7'2"
W.C.	2.2 x 1.2m / 7'2" x 3'11"
Living Room	4.3 x 3.6m / 14'1" x 11'9"
Family Room	4.5 x 3.5 m / 14'9" x 11'5"
Kitchen	4.0 x 3.2m / 13'1" x 10'5"
Dining	4.4 x 3.1m / 14'5" x 10'2"
Utility	2.1 x 1.6m / 6'10" x 5'2"
Study	3.8 x 2.7m / 12'5" x 8'10"
Landing	5.6 x 1.1m / 18'4" x 3'7"
Bathroom	3.1 x 3.0m / 10'2" x 9'10"
Bedroom 01	5.5 x 4.0m / 18'5" x 13'1"
En-Suite	2.3 x 1.6m / 7'6" x 5'2"
Wardrobe	2.3 x 1.6m / 7'6" x 5'2"
Bedroom 02	4.1 x 3.8m / 13'5" x 12'5"
Bedroom 03	3.7 x 2.7m / 12'1" x 8'10"
Bedroom 04	4.1 x 2.5m / 13'5" x 8'2"

AREA

203.4 sq. m. / 2,189.3 sq. ft.

FRONTAGE

13.7 m. / 44.9 ft.

Nothing is excluded from this impressive two-storey dwelling. The open plan area inside combines spectacularly well with the elegant features on the outside.

House D-116

See page 104 to order this design by post.

Ground floor plan

First floor plan

Hallway	3.0 x 2.9m / 14'5" x 9'6"
W.C.	1.7 x 1.5m / 5'6" x 4'11"
Study	3.1 x 3.0m / 10'2" x 9'10"
Playroom	5.1 x 4.0m / 16'8" x 13'1"
Utility	2.8 x 2.2m / 9'2" x 7'2"
W.C.	2.2 x 0.9m / 7'2" x 2'11"
Kitchen/Dining	5.9 x 5.0m / 19'4" x 16'4"
Living	5.5 x 4.2m / 18'5" x 13'9"
Bedroom 04	3.9 x 2.7m / 12'9" x 8'10"
Landing	5.2 x 1.5m / 17'1" x 4'11"
Bathroom	3.0 x 2.6m / 9'10" x 8'6"
Hot Press	1.5 x 1.3m / 4'11" x 4'3"
Bedroom 01	6.1 x 4.0m / 20' x 13'1"
Bedroom 02	6.1 x 4.3m / 20' x 14'1"
Bedroom 03	4.9 x 3.0m / 16'1" x 9'10"

AREA
224.3 sq. m. / 2,414.3 sq. ft.

FRONTAGE (including dining)
13.5m. / 44.2 ft.

The simple and elegant exterior of this dormer contrasts with the extent of space and rooms internally. The high pitch to the roof both adds significantly to the understated elegance and in addition provides a large amount of height to the first floor area compared to most dormers.

See page 104 to order this design by post.

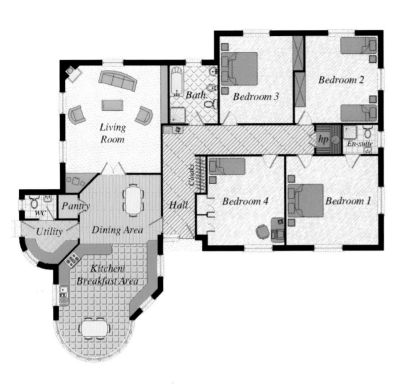

Floor plan

Hallway	6.0 x 1.8m / 19'8" x 5'10"
Dining Area	4.4 x 3.8m / 14'5" x 12'5"
Kitchen Area	6.2 x 5.6m / 20'3" x 18'4"
Utility	3.0 x 2.4m / 9'10" x 7'10"
W.C.	1.8 x 1.3m / 5'10" x 4'3"
Pantry	1.3 x 1.1m / 4'3" x 3'7"
Living Room	5.9 x 5.4m / 19'4" x 17'8"
Bathroom	3.2 x 2.7m / 10'5" x 8'10"
Hot Press	1.6 x 1.4m / 5'2" x 4'7"
Bedroom 01	5.2 x 4.9m / 17'1" x 16'1"
En-Suite	2.0 x 1.6m / 6'6" x 5'2"
Bedroom 02	4.8 x 4.7m / 15'8" x 15'5"
Bedroom 03	4.8 x 4.1m / 15'8" x 13'5"
Bedroom 04	4.9 x 4.3m / 16'1" x 14'1"

AREA
220.7 sq. m. / 2,375.6 sq. ft.

FRONTAGE (including utility)
20.5 m. / 67.3 ft.

This pretty design can be quite deceptive due to the amount of space available internally in relation to the compact front. The substantial utility would especially suit a family that spends a large amount of time outdoors.

Designing a garden depends on many factors; the following does not explain how to design a garden but to make the reader aware of what is involved.

- Compile a brief: Assessing the situation before starting.

THE SITE

The style of the house. This can be reflected in the garden. The boundaries - hedges, walls and fences, assess their condition and suitability. Orientation - Find the north point, follow the suns path through the day and at each season.

THE ELEMENTS

Note which parts of the garden are exposed and which are sheltered.

Views - Views from windows are important as we spend a lot of time looking out into the garden. Make a note of views to be retained and those that need screening.

Size and shape - The site plan is included as part of the documents , this will give a guideline to shape.

Levels - Is the garden flat? Is it sloping away from the house or towards it? Are the slopes gentle or steep? Levels do not need to be a problem, a steep site can be an opportunity for a water feature.

THE HUMAN FACTOR

How many people live in the house and from what age group do they comprise?

Do you have pets?

How will the garden be used? - Entertaining, play, relaxation, food production, hobbies, pottering around.

How much time will be spent in the garden for leisure and for maintenance?

THE PRACTICALITIES

Everyday items.

An outside tap is essential for watering plants.

Storage - Location of shed and/or greenhouse.

The washing line - Is it to be seen or unseen?

The bin - To be within easy access from the house and to collection point, yet not to be noticeable.

Fuel store i.e.) Coal, wood, turf, etc. - easy access is required. Careful thought is required to the location of the boiler house and oil tank so that it does not become an eyesore at a later date.

The compost heap - Every garden should have one to cut down on excess waste.

PERSONAL TASTE

Look at books, magazines and watch garden/design television programmes for ideas.

Visit garden centres and exhibitions.

Visit other peoples gardens both public and private. Take photographs, notes and sketches.

Take note of what style you like, preferred materials, favourite plants, pleasing shapes, textures and colours.

PROGRAMME OR WORK / BUDGET

Creating the garden

The budget - be realistic, set aside a percentage of the cost of the house to use in the garden. The garden is an outdoor room, think of it as an investment.

Is the work carried out in one go or over a period of years? A project can be phased to suit the budget. An on site builder can do a lot of the hardworks. In a large area, planting can be carried out over a number of seasons.

- Good preparation is the key to a successful garden

CLEARING THE SITE

Dispose rubbish in a skip or to a Council tip.

Vegetation that is overgrown and beyond remedial work, scrub, brambles and ivy should be removed including roots to give a clean site.

If you have existing mature trees in a vulnerable position or you suspect have a disease, consult a qualified tree surgeon who will carry out a report and safely remove any trees including the stump if necessary. The tree surgeon will also prune any mature trees that need a general overhaul to improve the structure of the tree.

Remove all rubbish i.e.) bricks, blocks, timbers, builders materials and any large stones.

Spray weeds using an approved weed killer as per manufacturers instructions or employ a trained person who holds a spraying certificate.

SOIL

Look at the soil profile, dig a hole 1m x 1m x 1m deep. This will show the depth of topsoil above the subsoil, which is noted by a colour and textual change. A good topsoil depth is 300mm. At a depth within the metre you may find the water table.

The ground may be holding water, this may be due to a compacted upper layer, this is common after building works. To remedy, break up the upper layer using a digger. If the lower layer is compacted a land drain may be required to help the excess water drain to a French drain/sump or to a surface water manhole.

Consult a land drainage specialist.

Test the soil to find its Ph level. If it is below 7 it is acid, if it's at 7 it is neutral and over 7 is alkaline. Before planting check that the plants chosen are suitable for the soil and position.

If the soil is light, the structure can be improved by incorporating composts and well-rotted manures to add humus and nutrients.

SERVICES

There is nothing worse than a manhole in an obvious position. This can be avoided by talking with your Architect and builder to locate positions of drains. The resulting manhole can be recessed so that it can blend into a path or a patio or sited well into a shrub bed.

Lighting and other electrics i.e. outside power points. Plan the circuits for outside at the same time as the house, decide on a point where the circuits enter the garden. The ducts need to be laid before any hardworks begin. The ducts need to be laid at the correct depth with warning tape laid above them. Use a qualified electrician to connect the cables.

Water i.e. outside taps - Lay piping during the hardworks to areas in the garden where water may be required. Use a qualified plumber for the connections.

Irrigation - If irrigation is required in raised planting beds or in shrub beds in paved areas, ducting can be laid underneath in the sub-base or through the wall construction to allow piping to be inserted later by an irrigation specialist. A position for a water tank will need to be considered during the design stage.

FOUNDATIONS AND SUB-BASES

All paving requires a hardcore sub-base, check manufacturers instructions for correct depth. The sub-base prevents sinking and subsidence and gives an even distribution of weight.

Edges require a concrete foundation and a haunch to prevent the edge from being dislodged.

Foundations for walls & retaining walls - The design of these need to be checked by an Engineer or Architect.

• The hardworks: The fixed elements

When choosing hard materials for the garden, look at the overall style of the house. Is it a period house, country/farm house, cottage, modern or a house with strong Architectural features? Look at the materials and the colour of the house and choose your materials to suit. A material element can be taken from the house and used in the garden e.g. A brick string course, stone used for quoins, granite for the sills, timber for cladding. Do not choose too many materials, as the overall effect will be cluttered.

Natural materials - Granite setts, sandstone, limestone.

Irish examples are Wicklow granite, Mayo sandstone, Donegal quartz and Liscannor stone.

Overseas examples include York stone, Portuguese granite setts, Indian sandstone.

Natural materials blend well into the garden, they are hard wearing and do not date. Granite setts look good as a raised edge between a driveway and a shrub bed. Stone flags should be laid in a random manner using flags with square corners and of varying sizes. Lay the flags with staggered joints to avoid chequerboard effect.

Brick - Reclaimed brick, old style new brick, and clay paving bricks. Bricks work well in an area where added warmth is required. Different bonding patterns can be achieved to add textual interest. Bricks can be mixed with natural materials to give relief to a large area. As an edging

they can be used either as a running or soldier course when laid flush or on end if the edge is raised,

Concrete products - Less expensive than natural materials, there are some good alternatives. Tobermore Tegula setts resemble granite setts, they are versatile and are good for creating patterns. These rumbled setts look natural compared to the paving block. The colour in concrete tends to fade, bear this in mind when colour matching. Concrete blocks are the mainstay of any wall, look on them as the structural element, they can be disguised by facing with brick or stone. The wall can be plastered and painted or rendered with a pigmented plaster. A good capping will help finish a dull wall.

Timber - Versatile in all planes of the garden.

Decking is popular as a means of extending the floor of the house into the garden. It is a useful way to deal with the changes in level from house to garden without building up levels of hardcore. Contact a specialist to design & build. Railway sleepers old and new give a solid, chunky effect to a retaining wall. Pressure treated timber edging is a very cheap alternative to brick or cobble to edge pathways.

Trellis latticework, arches and pergolas, used separately or combined add a decorative and functional element to the garden. Trellis will cover unsightly walls, give additional height to a boundary, be used as a division within the garden. Trellis is a structure on which climbing plants will grow. Arches form an entranceway into garden rooms. A pergola can be used to walk through as a tunnel of foliage, it can help give a sense of scale in a large space. It will screen buildings to give overhead cover.

•Structural Planting: The garden framework
TREES - Have a variety of uses.

A vertical element in a flat plane.

A screen to hide unsightly buildings and views.

As a specimen, feature or a centrepiece.

Encourage bird life with food, nest sites and perches.

Bring diversity with seasonal colour, flowers, leaf shape and fruits.

The number of trees to plant depends upon the size of garden and species chosen. Check the ultimate height, spread, longevity and growth rate of a particular species to see if it is suitable for your garden. An Oak tree is slow growing, lives to a mature age and will ultimately get too large for an average garden. Compared to a Birch tree, which is fast growing and is light in its structure to be tolerated in the average garden. Do not plant trees too close to buildings,

walls & hedges because of damage by roots and branch growth. Every garden should have at least one tree.

LARGE SHRUBS - In the garden give the main framework.

What is required is a balance of evergreens, shrubs with a coloured bark and shrubs that will give a contrast of foliage.

Evergreen shrubs are useful in the winter, as a backdrop for ornamental plants in the intervening months and for massing in areas that require shelter i.e. Prunus lusitanica (Portuguese laurel).

Large shrubs with coloured bark & twigs are also useful in the winter months for mass planting to give a bold effect i.e.) Cornus alba 'Siberica' (Dogwood).

Large deciduous shrubs with a contrast in leaf colour can be used to associate with other plants i.e. Cotinus coggygria 'Royal Purple', this shrub has a purple leaf.

Large shrubs can be used as features i.e. Cotoneaster 'Cornubia', Cornus contraversa 'Variegata'.

Large shrubs can accentuate points in a garden like an exclamation mark i.e. Piitosporum tenuifolium.

HEDGES

A hedge gives a definition as a boundary, use instead of a wall or fence as it is softer in appearance, has seasonal variation and the height can be altered.

A hedge can divide a garden internally to create outdoor rooms of different character or to shorten a long garden.

Low hedging to front borders i.e.) Buxus sempervirens (Box) Lavandula species (Lavender).

The surroundings: When deciding on a hedging species, consider the following:

In the countryside an indigenous mix will blend in i.e. Beech, Hawthorn & Holly.

Beside the sea with salt laden winds, Griselinia, Olearia & Escallonia will tolerate the conditions.

In a formal setting use Box, Yew, and Portuguese laurel.

For screening and shelter choose varieties that are evergreen like Prunus laurocerasus and Viburnum tinus.

CLIMBERS - Play an important role in the garden as they provide a vertical plane of growth.

Climbers hide unsightly walls, sheds and buildings. For example, concrete block walls can be covered using Virginia creeper, variegated Ivy or a climbing Hydrangea, all of these climbers are self-clinging and require no support. To cover large sheds, grow a rambling rose i.e. Rosa 'Kiftsgate'.

Climbers decorate and embellish surfaces particularly those covered with trellis and supporting wires so that the twining climbers have something to grow onto i.e. Clematis hybrids, honeysuckle and vines.

Wall shrubs can act like a climber, many shrubs can be grown against a wall and will benefit for its added protection i.e. Ceanothus species, Garrya elliptica, Pyracantha species & Fremontodendron.

• Features in the garden that can be incorporated as part of the overall picture

THE USE OF WATER

There is nothing like the sound of water to sooth or invigorate.

A water feature can be used in a variety of ways:

A focal point to attract the eye i.e. a geyser fountain.

As a reflection in a still pond.

As a vertical element, making use of level changes as a cascade.

To encourage wildlife, a nature pond with gentle banks and marginal planting.

A simple trickle, a bubble fountain over pebbles can be used as an incidental feature in a seating area. This is a good idea if safety issues surrounding water are a problem. The water is underground in a reservoir and is protected with a mesh.

A wall can be used for an in-situ wall fountain like a lion's head to spout water into a pool

Water introduces another medium for planting, moisture loving marginals and deep-water aquatics like water lilies.

If you have decided to put in a water feature, contact a specialist as an aesthetic eye is required especially for natural looking streams and ponds.

CONTAINERS - A good selection of pots and containers are invaluable.

A large urn can be used as a focal point to end a vista.

A large deep container for climbing plants if it is not possible to plant into the soil adjacent to a house.

Group lots of pots of varying sizes on the patio and near the house. There are a good variety of pots available at garden centres, make sure that they are frost proof.

Pots are handy for seasonal variation. It is easier to change plants in a pot than to change a whole scheme in a garden. The group of pots can give a splash of colour when the rest of the garden is quiet.

Pots are a good way to show off bulbs & annuals and a practical way to keep herbs.

ARTWORK

Artwork can be bought off the shelf or as commissioned pieces.

The piece can be for a particular position as a focal point i.e. Sculpture at the end of a path with planting at the base.

To decorate a bare wall, compile a mosaic or a mural. These can be embellished with climbing plants and trellis.

In an interactive situation like a fountain, where the water is directed by the sculpture. Traditional elements such as a garden seat or a sundial can be creatively transformed into art.

The possibility of using different materials i.e. Glass, metal, stone will enhance the richness of the garden.

Art can be subtly hidden amongst planting as incidentals that will give an element of surprise.

It is recommended to consult with a garden designer when planning the garden, even in the early stages when the Architects plans are being developed.

This article was kindly submitted by Lisa Murphy who has her own practise, Landscape Restoration Design Ltd in conjunction with Andrew Glenn-Craigie. Lisa can be contacted at The Rookery, Powerstown, Clonee, Dublin 15. Tel. 01- 821 7046. She has a Degree and Diploma in Landscape Architecture and is a full member of the GLDA.

House Designs over 2,500 sq. ft.

Shut the door. Not that it lets in the cold but that it lets out the cosiness.

Mark Twain (1835 - 1910). American writer.

House E-101

See page 104 to order this design by post.

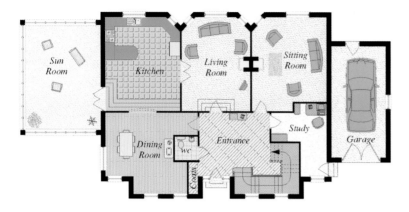

Ground floor plan

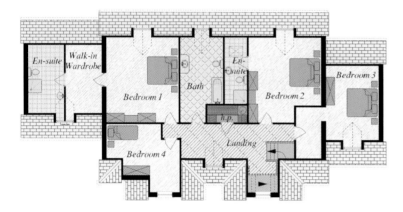

First floor plan

Hallway	4.5 x 4.1m / 14'9" x 13'5"
W.C.	1.7 x 1.0m / 5'6" x 3'3"
Dining Room	5.2 x 5.2m / 17'1" x 17'1"
Kitchen	5.8 x 5.0m / 19'3" x 16'4"
Sun Room	6.5 x 5.0m / 21'3" x 16'4"
Living Room	5.8 x 4.6m / 19'3" x 15'1"
Sitting Room	6.0 x 5.0m / 19'8" x 16'4"
Study	4.5 x 1.8m / 14'9" x 5'10"
Garage	6.9 x 3.6m / 22'7" x 11'9"
Landing	7.5 x 2.3m / 24'7" x 7'6"
Bathroom	5.4 x 3.0m / 17'8" x 9'10"
Hot Press	2.6 x 1.2m / 8'6" x 3'11"
Bedroom 01	5.4 x 5.0m / 17'8" x 16'4"
En-suite	4.3 x 2.5m / 14'1" x 8'2"
Wardrobe	4.3 x 2.5m / 14'1" x 8'2"
Bedroom 02	5.4 x 5.0m / 17'8" x 16'4"
En-suite	4.2 x 1.6m / 13'9" x 5'2"
Bedroom 03	4.7 x 3.6m / 15'5" x 11'9"
Bedroom 04	4.8 x 3.4m / 15'8" x 11'2"

AREA(excluding garage)
343.7 sq. m. / 3,699 sq. ft.
FRONTAGE
24.0 m. / 78.7 ft.

This elegant dormer offers extensive space and light with a relatively low ridge height. A large site would be essential for such an elongated frontage.

House E-102

See page 102 for plan prices.

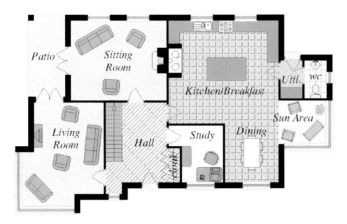

Ground floor plan

First floor plan

Hallway	4.1 x 3.4m / 13'5" x 11'2"
Living Room	5.4 x 3.9m / 17'8" x 12'9"
Sitting Room	5.1 x 4.3m / 16'8" x 14'1"
Patio	4.2 x 2.1m / 13'9" x 6'10"
Kitchen	5.8 x 5.5m / 19'3" x 18'5"
Dining Room	3.0 x 3.0m / 9'10" x 9'10"
Sun Area	2.5 x 2.4m / 8'2" x 7'10"
Utility	2.4 x 2.1m / 7'10" x 6'10"
Study	2.9 x 2.1m / 9'6" x 6'10"
Landing	5.8 x 1.5m / 19'3" x 4'11"
Bathroom	2.7 x 2.7m / 8'10" x 8'10"
Hot Press	1.3 x 1.4m / 4'3" x 4'7"
Bedroom 01	5.6 x 5.0m / 18'4" x 16'4"
En-suite	3.4 x 2.6m / 11'2" x 8'6"
Wardrobe	2.4 x 1.6m / 7'10" x 5'2"
Bedroom 02	5.6 x 3.7m / 18'4" x 12'1"
Bedroom 03	4.6 x 4.4m / 15'1" x 14'5"
Bedroom 04	4.0 x 3.9m / 13'1" x 12'9"

AREA
233.2 sq. m. / 2,510 sq. ft.

FRONTAGE
17.1 m. / 58.10 ft.

This extensive family home offers four large double rooms in the upstairs area. A breakfast area adjacent to the kitchen is proving increasingly to be the norm in Irish households.

House E-103

Phone Lo-Call 1890 713 713 to order plans by credit card.

Ground floor plan

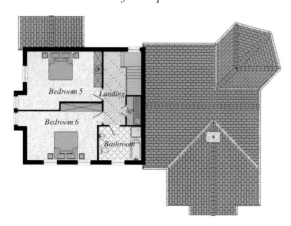

First floor plan

Hallway	3.6 x 3.6m / 11'9" x 11'9"
Kitchen	5.2 x 4.5m / 17'1" x 14'9"
Dining Room	6.4 x 3.7m / 20'11" x 12'1"
Utility	2.5 x 2.3m / 8'2" x 7'6"
W.C.	2.1 x 1.1m / 6'10" x 3'7"
Living Room	5.8 x 4.6m / 19' x 15'1"
Bedroom 01	5.0 x 4.4m / 16'4" x 14'5"
En-suite	1.9 x 2.0m / 6'2" x 6'6"
Wardrobe	1.9 x 1.8m / 6'2" x 5'10"
Bedroom 02	3.8 x 3.7m / 12'5" x 12'1"
Bedroom 03	3.4 x 2.7m / 11'2" x 8'10"
Bedroom 04	4.2 x 2.4m / 13'9" x 7'10"
Landing	5.3 x 1.8m / 17'4" x 5'10"
Bathroom	3.2 x 2.6m / 10'5" x 8'6"
Hot Press	2.0 x 1.2m / 6'6" x 3'11"
Bedroom 05	5.6 x 3.8m / 18'4" x 12'5"
Bedroom 06	5.3 x 3.7m / 17'4" x 12'1"

AREA
240.5 sq. m. / 2,590 sq. ft.

FRONTAGE
17.8 m. / 58.3 ft.

Many elements are included in this elegant family home. Wall / roof windows as shown are becoming a very popular feature.

House E-104

Phone 00 353 56 71300 to order plans by credit card from outside the Republic of Ireland.

Ground floor plan

First floor plan

Hallway	6.4 x 2.6m / 20'1" x 8'6"
Living Room	6.4 x 4.8m / 20'1" x 15'8"
Family Room	5.4 x 4.0m / 17'8" x 13'1"
Utility	4.1 x 2.3m / 13'5" x 7'6"
W.C.	2.6 x 1.2m / 8'6" x 3'11"
Kitchen/Dining	9.2 x 4.0m / 31'6" x 13'1"
Garage	6.8 x 3.3m / 22'3" x 10'9"
Landing	8.9 x 1.0m / 30'7" x 3'3"
Bathroom	2.5 x 2.1m / 8'2" x 6'10"
Hot Press	1.8 x 0.9m / 5'10" x 2'11"
Bedroom 01	5.6 x 5.4m / 18'4" x 17'8"
En-Suite	2.7 x 1.9m / 8'10" x 6'2"
Bedroom 02	3.5 x 3.3m / 11'5" x 10'9"
Bedroom 03	4.8 x 2.5m / 15'8" x 8'2"
Bedroom 04	5.2 x 4.2m / 17'1" x 13'9"

AREA (excluding garage)
233.5 sq. m. / 2,513.3 sq. ft.

Frontage (including garage)
19.7m / 64.6 ft.

Sharp lines and extensive glazing are the two main features of this impressive dwelling. A combined kitchen / dining area, has become the norm within the last number of years, and it is often a good idea to separate these visually with different coverings to the floor surfaces e.g. tiles and timber.

House E-105

See page 104 to order this design by post.

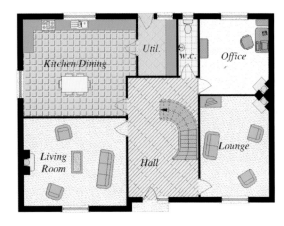

Ground floor plan

First floor plan

Hallway	6.5 x 4.0m / 21'3" x 13'1"
Living Room	5.8 x 4.8m / 19'3" x 15'8"
Kitchen/Dining	6.4 x 5.3m / 20'1" x 17'4"
Utility	3.1 x 2.2m / 10'2" x 7'2"
W.C.	3.1 x 1.1m / 10'2" x 3'7"
Office	4.1 x 3.1m / 13'5" x 10'2"
Lounge	5.5 x 3.9m / 18'5" x 12'9"
Landing	6.8 x 1.8m / 22'3" x 5'10"
Bathroom	2.8 x 2.7m / 9'2" x 8'10"
Hot Press	2.7 x 1.3m / 8'10" x 4'3"
Bedroom 01	5.8 x 5.3m / 19'3" x 17'4"
En-suite	2.8 x 1.9m / 9'2" x 6'2"
Bedroom 02	5.8 x 4.2m / 19'3" x 13'9"
Bedroom 03	4.7 x 3.9m / 15'5" x 12'9"
Bedroom 04	4.9 x 3.2m / 16'1" x 10'5"

AREA
275.4 sq. m. / 2,964.3 sq. ft.

FRONTAGE
14.5 m. / 47.6 ft.

This elegant family home shows the popular tudor style. The access to the downstairs toilet is from the hallway in this case, in order to facilitate the office, but may be changed if desired to the utility.

House E-106

See page 102 for plan prices.

Ground floor plan

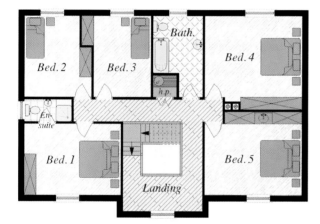

First floor plan

Hallway	4.8 x 4.3m / 15'8" x 14'1"
Kitchen/Dining	5.9 x 4.9m / 19'4" x 16'1"
Garage	5.0 x 2.7m / 16'4" x 8'10"
W.C.	1.5 x 1.5m / 4'11" x 4'11"
Living Room	5.2 x 4.5m / 17'1" x 14'9"
Play Room	1.9 x 2.6m / 6'2" x 8'6"
Family Room	5.8 x 4.1m / 19'3" x 13'5"
Landing	5.5 x 4.0m / 18'5" x 13'1"
Bathroom	4.0 x 2.5m / 13'1" x 8'2"
Hot Press	1.2 x 1.1m / 3'11" x 3'7"
Bedroom 01	4.9 x 3.5m / 16'1" x 11'5"
En-Suite	2.4 x 1.1m / 7'10" x 3'7"
Bedroom 02	4.0 x 3.4m / 13'1" x 11'2"
Bedroom 03	4.0 x 2.9m / 13'1" x 9'6"
Bedroom 04	4.9 x 4.6m / 16'1" x 15'1"
Bedroom 05	4.9 x 4.1m / 16'1" x 13'5"

AREA (excluding garage)
233.1 sq. m. / 2,509 sq. ft.

FRONTAGE
14.6 m. / 47.9 ft.

A number of styles, Irish farmhouse among others come together to form this fabulous dormer style dwelling. The amount of space is especially advantageous to the upstairs, where five bedrooms can be accommodated.

House E-107

Phone 00 353 56 71300 to order plans by credit card from outside the Republic of Ireland.

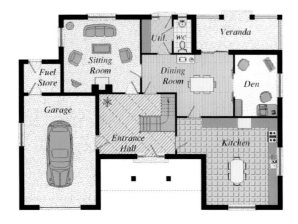

Ground floor plan

First floor plan

Hallway	5.0 x 3.8m / 16'4" x 12'5"
Garage	6.9 x 4.7m / 22'7" x 15'5"
Fuel	2.4 x 1.8m / 17'8" x 14'5"
Sitting Room	5.0 x 4.6m / 16'4" x 15'1"
Utility	2.1 x 2.0m / 6'10" x 6'6"
W.C.	2.1 x 1.2m / 6'10" x 3'11"
Veranda	5.4 x 1.9m / 17'8" x 6'2"
Dining	6.0 x 3.9m / 19'8" x 12'9"
Den	3.9 x 2.8m / 12'9" x 9'2"
Kitchen	5.5 x 4.7m / 18'5" x 15'5"
Landing	3.7 x 2.7m / 12'1" x 8'10"
Bathroom	4.1 x 2.7m / 13'5" x 8'10"
Hot Press	2.1 x 1.6m / 6'10" x 5'2"
Bedroom 01	6.0 x 4.7m / 19'8" x 15'5"
En-Suite	2.8 x 2.5m / 9'2" x 8'2"
Bedroom 02	3.7 x 3.3m / 12'1" x 10'9"
Bedroom 03	4.3 x 3.3m / 14'1" x 10'9"
Bedroom 04	5.3 x 3.9m / 17'4" x 12'9"
Bedroom 05	5.5 x 4.7m / 18'5" x 15'5"
En-Suite	2.8 x 2.1m / 9'2" x 6'10"

AREA (excluding garage)
267.7 sq. m. / 2,881.4 sq. ft.
FRONTAGE (including dining)
 17.2m. / 56.4 ft.

Elegance and simplicity are the key-words with this beautiful design, both internally and externally. All major habitable rooms are easily accessible to each other.

Phone Lo-Call 1890 713 713 to order plans by credit card.

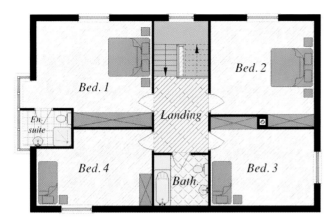

Ground floor plan

First floor plan

Lobby	2.4 x 2.0m / 7'10" x 6'6"
Hallway	4.5 x 3.9m / 14'9" x 12'9"
Office	4.5 x 4.4m / 14'9" x 14'5"
Family Room	5.6 x 4.1m / 18'4" x 13'5"
Hot Press	2.3 x 1.1m / 7'6" x 3'7"
Kitchen/Dining	8.6 x 5.0m / 28'2" x 16'4"
Utility	3.3 x 1.7m / 10'9" x 5'6"
W.C.	1.5 x 1.5m / 4'11" x 4'11"
Living Room	6.1 x 5.8m / 20' x 19'3"
Landing	3.5 x 2.6m / 11'5" x 8'6"
Bathroom	2.6 x 2.4m / 8'6" x 7'10"
Bedroom 01	5.6 x 5.0m / 18'4" x 16'4"
En-suite	2.4 x 1.7m / 7'10" x 5'6"
Bedroom 02	5.0 x 4.4m / 16'4" x 14'5"
Bedroom 03	5.0 x 4.2m / 16'4" x 13'9"
Bedroom 04	5.6 x 3.6m / 18'4" x 11'9"

AREA
288.9 sq. m. / 3,109.7 sq. ft.

FRONTAGE (excluding utility)
14.0 m. / 45.9 ft.

This amazing two-storey has a range of features. The stunning ground floor contrasts perfectly with the simpler but more practical first floor.

House E-109

Phone 00 353 56 71300 to order plans by credit card from outside the Republic of Ireland.

Ground floor plan

First floor plan

Lobby	2.4 x 1.8m / 7'10" x 5'10"
Coats	1.8 x 1.3m / 5'10" x 4'3"
Hallway	3.8 x 3.8m / 12'5" x 12'5"
Family Room	5.4 x 4.2m / 17'8" x 13'9"
Living Room	7.5 x 5.6m / 24'7" x 18'4"
Utility	3.2 x 2.3m / 10'5" x 7'6"
W.C.	2.0 x 1.5m / 6'6" x 4'11"
Pantry	1.5 x 1.1m / 4'11" x 3'7"
Kitchen	5.9 x 4.8m / 19'4" x15'8"
Dining Room	4.0 x 3.6m / 13'1" x 11'9"
Landing	4.8 x 3.9m / 15'8" x 12'9"
Bathroom	2.9 x 2.7m / 9'6" x 8'10"
Hot Press	1.9 x 1.5m / 6'2" x 4'11"
Master Bedroom	6.0 x 4.8m / 19'8" x 15'8"
En-Suite	2.4 x 1.8m / 7'10" x 5'10"
Wardrobe	3.6 x 1.5m / 11'9" x 4'11"
Bedroom 02	4.8 x 3.9m / 15'8" x 12'9"
Bedroom 03	3.1 x 3.1m / 10'2" x 10'2"
Bedroom 04	4.8 x 3.7m / 15'8" x 12'1"
En-Suite	1.9 x 1.6m / 6'2" x 5'2"
Bedroom 05	3.6 x 3.0m / 11'9" x 9'10"

AREA

283.7 sq. m. / 3,053.7 sq. ft.

FRONTAGE 15.6m. / 51.8 ft.

Impressive is the word that most springs to mind when viewing this spectacular two-storey. The arch between kitchen and dining was included to ensure usability for the latter, however, many people replace this feature with double doors.

House E-110

See page 104 to order this design by post.

Ground floor plan

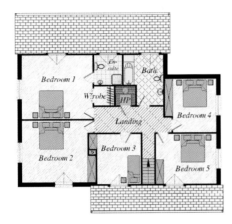

First floor plan

Hallway	6.0 x 4.1m / 19'8" x 13'5"
Living Room	5.8 x 4.4m / 19'3" x 14'5"
Dining Room	4.7 x 3.8m / 15'5" x 12'5"
Kitchen	6.1 x 4.7m / 20' x 15'5"
Utility	3.0 x 2.5m / 9'10" x 8'2"
W.C.	2.2 x 1.2m / 7'2" x 3'11"
Family Room	4.6 x 4.3m / 15'1" x 14'1"
Sitting Room	4.8 x 4.6m / 15'8" x 15'1"
Landing	5.8 x 1.8m / 19'3" x 5'10"
Bathroom	3.7 x 3.0m / 12'1" x 9'10"
Hot Press	1.5 x 1.4m / 4'11" x 4'7"
Bedroom 01	5.4 x 4.7m / 17'8" x 15'5"
En-Suite	2.2 x 2.1m / 7'2" x 6'10"
Wardrobe	1.5 x 1.4m / 4'11" x 4'7"
Bedroom 02	5.6 x 4.6m / 18'4" x 15'1"
Bedroom 03	3.7 x 3.3m / 12'1" x 10'9"
Bedroom 04	3.9 x 3.9m / 12'9" x 12'9"
Bedroom 05	4.6 x 3.7m / 15'1" x 12'1"

AREA
281.7 sq. m. / 3,032.1 sq. ft.
FRONTAGE
15.3m. / 50.1 ft.

An American style veranda is one of the many features of this superb dormer. One of the many advantages of this dwelling is the large amount of light afforded to all rooms.

House E-111

See page 102 for plan prices.

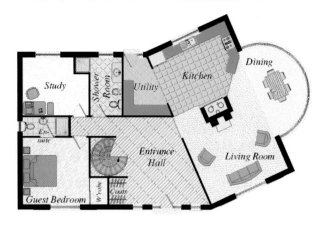

Ground floor plan

First floor plan

Hallway	5.1 x 5.0m / 16'8" x 16'4"
Guest Bedroom	4.0 x 3.9m / 13'1" x 12'9"
En-suite	2.8 x 1.1m / 9'2" x 3'7"
Study	4.0 x 3.9m / 13'1" x 12'9"
Shower Room	3.4 x 1.9m / 11'2" x 6'2"
Utility	3.4 x 2.9m / 11'2" x 9'6"
Kitchen/Living	9.5 x 5.1m / 31'1" x 16'18"
Dining	5.3 x 2.8m / 17'4" x 9'2"
Landing	4.6 x 1.1m / 15'1" x 3'7"
Bathroom	3.4 x 3.4m / 11'2" x 11'2"
Hot Press	1.8 x 0.9m / 5'10" x 2'11"
Bedroom 01	5.6 x 5.1m / 18'4" x 16'8"
En-suite	3.7 x 2.5m / 12'1" x 8'2"
Wardrobe	3.7 x 2.5m / 12'1" x 8'2"
Balcony	5.3 x 2.8m / 17'4" x 9'2"
Bedroom 02	5.5 x 3.4m / 18'5" x 11'2"
En-suite	1.8 x 1.8m / 5'10" x 5'10"
Bedroom 03	4.0 x 3.6m / 13'1" x 11'9"
Bedroom 04	4.9 x 3.9m / 16'1" x 12'9"

AREA (excluding balcony)
267.5 sq. m. / 2,879.3 sq. ft.
FRONTAGE (excluding dining)
16.8m. / 55.1 ft.

Reminiscent of a French country house, this delightful two-storey offers a wealth of extras. The centrally located fireplace / cooker allows for unrestricted access and ease of movement around the key habitable areas.

House E-112

Phone Lo-Call 1890 713 713 to order plans by credit card.

Ground floor plan

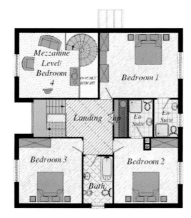

First floor plan

Hallway	5.9 x 2.0m / 19'4" x 6'6"
Living Room	4.3 x 4.3m / 14'1" x 14'1"
Study	5.4 x 4.4m / 17'8" x 14'5"
W.C.	1.5 x 1.5m / 4'11" x 4'11"
Porch	2.6 x 1.5m / 8'6" x 4'11"
Kitchen	4.4 x 3.7m / 14'5" x 12'1"
Dining	4.4 x 3.4m / 14'5" x 11'2"
Family Room	4.4 x 3.4m / 14'5" x 11'2"
Landing	3.7 x 2.0m / 12'1" x 6'6"
Bathroom	3.2 x 2.0m / 10'5" x 6'6"
Hot Press	2.5 x 0.9m / 8'2" x 2'11"
Bedroom 01	5.4 x 4.4m / 17'8" x 14'5"
En-Suite	2.5 x 1.7m / 8'2" x 5'6"
Bedroom 02	4.4 x 4.4m / 14'5" x 14'5"
En-Suite	2.5 x 1.6m / 8'2" x 5'2"
Bedroom 03	4.4 x 4.4m / 14'5" x 14'5"
Bedroom 04	4.4 x 4.2m / 14'5" x 13'9"

AREA
238.6 sq. m. / 2,568.2 sq. ft.

FRONTAGE (including dining)
11.5m. / 37.7 ft.

This modern classic is often used on a restricted site due to its relatively shortened façade length. More or less everything required in a dwelling is incorporated in its neat internal layout, take note of the very popular spiral staircase and mezzanine area over the study area.

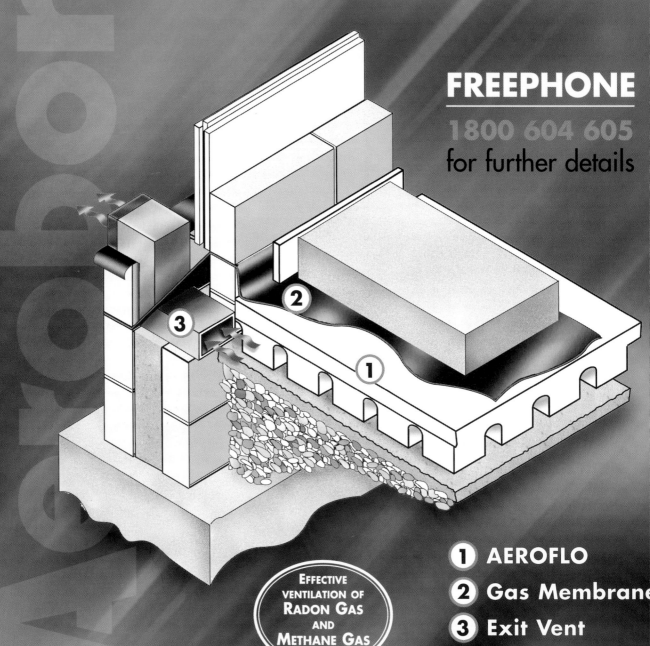

Cosy but not Costly

It's nice to know with a little knowledge and just a little effort you can achieve a cosy comfortable home, saving energy and helping our fragile environment.

With today's new building technology and mandatory standards in new homes, buyers can be well satisfied with improvements, both in comfort levels and energy costs. However, there are many ways to improve this performance, increasing your comfort level and reducing heating and energy bills.

Let's consider what you get when you buy your new house and help you to appreciate how your new house is insulated.

Ground floors are difficult to insulate after completion; therefore it is essential and cost effective to insulate to a higher level during the construction stage. Solid floor slabs i.e. concrete will require under floor insulation. The insulation most commonly used is expanded polystyrene insulation typically 55mm thick, laid under the concrete floor slab. 2003 proposed building regulations will dramatically increase the thermal value and substantially reduce heat loss.

Walls, depending on how they are constructed, rely on various tried and tested methods of insulation to increase their thermal efficiency. With cavity walls, where there are two separate leaves of blockwork or outer leaf of brick cavity wall insulation is placed against the outer face of the inner leaf in the cavity, leaving an all important residual gap of minimum 40mm. Where hollow block walls are used (Dublin/Kildare area), the insulation is placed on the inside face, either by friction fitting between treated timber battens or bonded to plasterboard panels. The most common insulation used is expanded polystyrene insulation and can vary from 60 - 100mm in a typical modern house. Once again if you decide on increased thickness you will certainly benefit from the enhanced performance.

Roofs for the most part are of pitched form, where a layer of insulation is laid between and/or over the ceiling joists. This is called a 'cold roof' where the space above the insulation is cold. Typically a layer of mineral wool quilt 150mm (6") is generally acceptable. However if two separate layers say 100mm (4") thick were installed, one layer between and one layer over the ceiling joists, a huge increase in performance can be achieved. Insulating the roof slope is now made easier with friction fitted expanded polystyrene panels that will provide ventilation over the insulation to prevent condensation forming. A vapour barrier placed on the warm side is essential in this instance.

Isn't it strange that car manufacturers openly state the comfort, environmental friendliness and fuel performance of their products (cars being the second biggest investment after house purchase for the average person) and the running costs of houses is rarely mentioned!

OUR TOP TIPS
• Insulate as much as you can afford when your home is being built.
• Buy your fuel in bulk if possible, as out of season rates can give useful savings.
• Fit an automatic time control switch to your boiler, and fit thermostatic control valves to individual room radiators.
• Do not heat unused rooms, keeping in mind that the temperature must not fall below 10°C (50 F)
• Provide a good quality carpet, particularly over suspended floors (a good carpet can deliver an insulation value equivalent to 25mm thickness of mineral wool insulation).
• Use hot water wisely, do not overfill the bath, and use a shower in place of a bath where possible.
• Make sure all your water pipes are well insulated especially in the attic area.
• Do not insulate under the cold water storage tank, let some heat up to avoid freezing. But do insulate the tank on all sides including the cover.
• Provide sufficient ventilation at roof eaves/soffit level to prevent condensation. This will mean the attic temperature will be considerably colder than the rest of the house at a lower level.
• Curtains provide good thermal insulation. Radiators should not be located behind drawn curtains.

Energy efficient houses are now recognised as both cost effective and environmentally friendly. Check the insulation is right before you buy or build.

Kindly submitted by Aerobord Ltd, Askeaton, Co .Limerick.

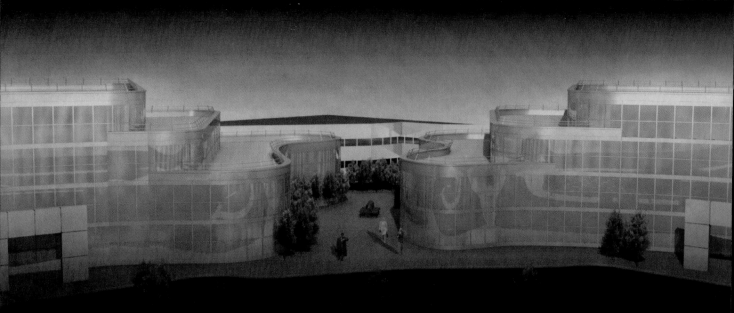

To see what we're all about,

1

2

3

4

1. BUILDING INTERIORS

2. OFFICE DEVELOPMENTS

3. DESIGN CONCEPTS

4. ENVIRONMENTAL IMPACT

simply turn the page...
and the next page...and the next page...and the ne...

In fact you can go to *any page in this book.* Using the latest 3D modelling software and more than a little expertise, the team at *Radius Technologies* have given form and life to the building plans featured in this book – showing you clearly what you could otherwise have only imagined.

Many a good idea has fallen by the wayside because it hasn't been articulated or represented clearly. In an architectural or planning environment that can be a costly waste. Our 3D modelling service brings raw ideas to life, presenting the idea to its full potential.

Office developments, schools, hotels, environmental impact studies...just some of the projects we've worked on in recent months. But the potential for 3D modelling goes way beyond that – indeed it's limited only by your imagination.

For further information on what we can do for you, contact our *Sales Team* today on 051 843861.
We'll be only too happy to help bring your idea to life.

MODELLING

radius>technologies

6 variations to add to your chosen plans - free of charge

To Adam, Paradise was home.
To the good among his descendants, home is paradise.
Julius Charles Hare (1795 - 1855). English translator.

Garage G-101

Garage   6.8m x 4.3m / 22'3" x 14'1"

A standard yet very effective garage. Extra width is provided in order to give some extra storage down the side.

Garage G-102

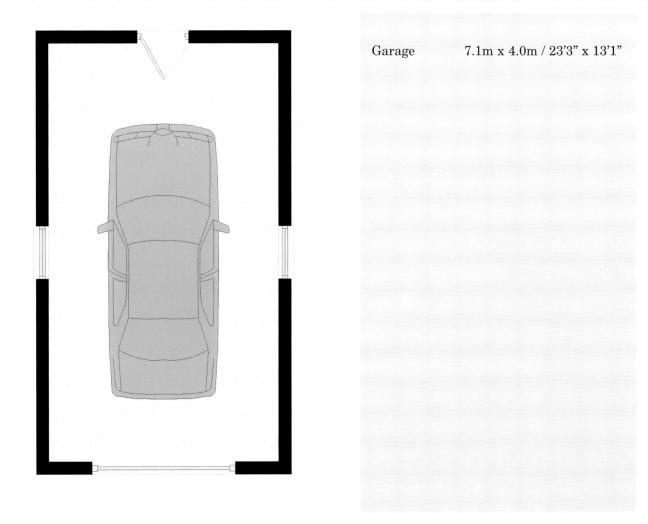

Garage   7.1m x 4.0m / 23'3" x 13'1"

This is basically a variation on garage G-101. The windows and door positions are however rearranged.

Your choice of Garage Plans free with all house plans purchased

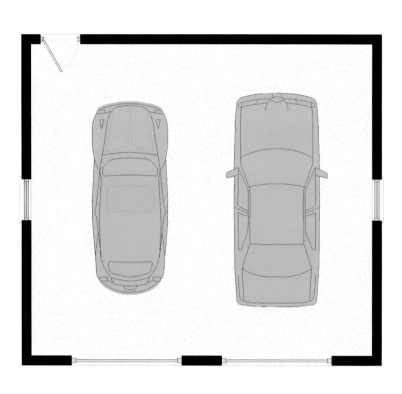

Car Space   7.7m x 6.8m / 25'2" x 22'3"

The classic double garage. This size of garage is becoming increasingly more and more popular.

Garage G-104

Your choice of Garage Plans free with all house plans purchased

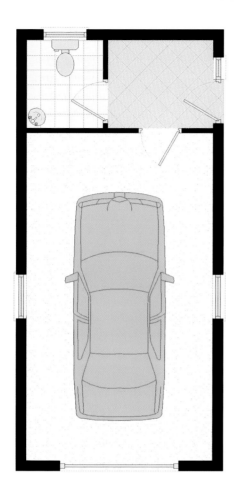

Car Space	6.7m x 3.9m	21'9" x 12'9"
Storage	2.2m x 1.8m	7'2" x 5'10"
W.C.	1.8m x 1.6m	5'10" x 5'2"

The storage and toilet space to the rear would prove especially useful to someone who spends a lot of time outdoors. We strongly recommend you match the materials and style of your garage with the main dwellinghouse, for uniformity.

Your choice of Garage Plans free with all house plans purchased

Car Space	7.0m x 3.9m / 22'11" x 12'9"
Storage	5.1m x 3.9m / 16'8" x 12'9"
Fuel	2.1m x 1.8m / 6'10" x 5'10"
W.C.	1.8m x 1.6m / 5'10" x 5'2"

The garage with everything! Work space, car space, storage and toilet are all provided in this large garage, and due to the high roof, many people utilise the attic spac

Garage G-106

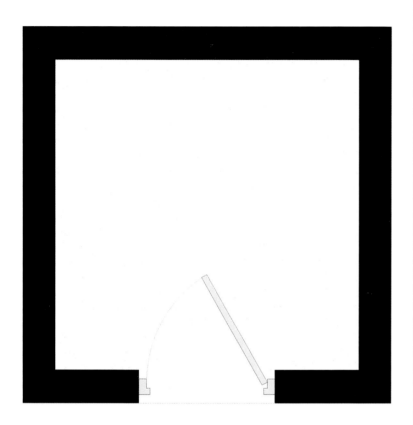

Burner Space   2.0m x 2.0m / 6'6" x 6'6"

Not really a garage but a boiler house! With modern construction you may choose to locate your fuel burner inside or outside the main dwellinghouse, and this type of construction perfectly suits the latter.

Planning Permission

The following are a list of the items required by each Local Authority in the Republic of Ireland, in order to lodge an official planning application. However, it is always advisable to seek advice, either directly from the planner in your relevant area, or alternatively, the Local County Development Plan, or similar publication.

Additionally, some extra information which might aid a planning officer to favour your application is always a good idea, e.g. details of family involvement in the area, business interests etc., and these can often be submitted as an attached hand written or typed note.

1. Signed and fully completed **application form.**

2. 2 copies of a **newspaper notice** as shown in the local/national paper. It is important to note that there is a deadline of two weeks from the date of publication of the newspaper to date of application submission.

3. 2 copies of the fully completed and signed **site notice.** Original to be erected on site for a minimum of 1 month, and visible to any passers by.

4. 4 copies of sections, elevations and **plans** of your house. Minimum scale 1:100 (as we provide).

5. 4 copies of the **specification** of your house. This involves some notes about the materials to be involved in the house, and in particular the finishes as to be seen, i.e. roof finish, wall finish etc. (as we provide).

6. 4 copies of a **site layout plan.** Minimum scale 1:500, which should show the entire site and any landscaping, driveways, septic tanks, boreholes, north point etc, involved in the site or surrounding sites. Also include some details of the relevant ''sight lines'', which basically are the visible distances which can be seen as you drive out of the site onto the public roadway. Very important to planners!

7. **Percolation/water table test results,** where a private effluent treatment system (i.e. septic tank), is to be used. It is important to note that different Local Authorities have varied requirements for this test, e.g. some authorities carry out the test themselves and charge a fee, some Local Authorities require the tester to have a certain level of Professional Indemnity Insurance.

8. **Planning Fee.** This currently stands at £47.00 per dwelling. However, this is reduced to £24.00 for approval applications (where outline planning permission has already been sought and acquired). It is important to note that there are additional fees for stables, commercial structures etc.

9. Scaled and marked **Site Location Map,** which should easily identify the position of your site in relation to the surrounding area. Don't forget such important items as north sign, ordnance survey number and details of any surrounding dwellings, rivers, etc.

Design Alterations

The following pages show how designs throughout this book can be altered to suit individual needs and tastes.

MK Home Design offers you the unique opportunity, if so desired of altering the finishes shown in this book, to suit your site or indeed your personal preferences. We have taken a design at random, House E-103, and show how a dwelling can be transformed with some thought and imagination.

In addition, it may be necessary to "flip over" or mirror the plans as shown in order to locate the key habitable areas: kitchen, dining etc. on the sunny side of the site. Again, this can be done free of charge. If your finish differs from that shown in our 3D image, please mark any changes legibly and clearly on the order form on page 104, or state clearly to our office when ordering by credit card. Be sure to include any important features such as arches over windows, plaster reveals etc., etc.

We begin below by having house E-103 (shown on page 78), flipped over and continue on the following pages with just some of the choices available.

House E-103 - mirror image

Brick Finish

Stone Finish

Plaster Finish

Tudor Finish

Plan Package Prices

Plan Type	Price	+VAT @ 20%	TOTAL
Section A (e.g. A-104)	IR£196.89 €250.00	IR£39.38 €50.00	**IR£236.27** **€300.00**
Section B	IR£216.58 €275.00	IR£43.32 €55.00	**IR£259.90** **€330.00**
Section C	IR£236.27 €300.00	IR£47.25 €60.00	**IR£285.52** **€360.00**
Section D	IR£255.96 €325.00	IR£51.19 €65.00	**IR£307.15** **€390.00**
Section E	IR£275.65 €350.00	IR£55.13 €70.00	**IR£330.78** **€420.00**

Prices shown are current at time of publication and include post and packaging worldwide. Allow up to seven days to delivery within Ireland upon receipt of payment.

What You Receive

1. 5 copies of the plans with general dimensions at a scale of 1:100 for planning application/discussion purposes.

2. 5 copies of the fully dimensioned working drawing plans at a scale of 1:50 for building contractors/construction purposes.

3. 5 copies of the working written specification for builders pricing and construction purposes.

4. 6 copies of fully dimensioned garage plans as chosen, if required. If this is left blank on the order form, it is assumed that garage plans are not required.

5. Two blank building contracts for you and your builder.

We can supply extra copies where and when required.
Please phone Lo-Call 1890 713 713 or 00 353 56 71300 for more information.

Specification

The following shall allow us to accurately describe the materials to be used in your house.

If nothing is written, it is assumed that the choice shown in italic in the right hand column is satisfactory, (standard, but of good quality).

External Wall Construction: .... *Standard 300mm cavity.*

Roof: .... *Fibre cement slates*

Stairs: .... *Red Deal.*

Windows: .... *White Double glazed uPVC/Georgian.*

Skirting and architraves: .... *White Deal.*

Internal Doors:: .... *Pine Four Panelled Engineered.*

Entrance Door: .... *Teak.*

Ground Floor: .... *Concrete*

Upper Floor Construction: .... *Timber*

Upper Floor Finish: .... *White Deal floorboards*

Fascia, soffit and barge: .... *White uPVC*

Heating System: .... *Oil Fired*

Garage:

Wall Construction: .... *9" block*

Wall Finish: .... *To match house*

Door: .... *Aluminium*

ADDITIONAL REMARKS

....

....

....

....

....

* A photocopy of this page is acceptable

Order Form

You may also phone Lo-Call 1890 713 713 or 00 353 56 71300 to give the information below and order by credit card and/or with any queries.
Don't forget to include the specification on the previous page.

Name:.. Contact Telephone No:.......................................

Home Address:...

....

Site Address (if applicable):...

....

PLAN NO. CHOSEN .... Mirror Plans: Yes   No

Wall Finish as shown on 3D image: Yes   No

If not, indicate finish to:

Front view: .... Side views:.......................................

Rear view: ....

GARAGE NO. CHOSEN .... Mirror Plans: Yes   No

Wall Finish to match main house: Yes   No

If not, indicate finish to:

Front view:.. Side views:.......................................

Rear view:...

Method of Payment: Cheque   Yes   No

Postal Order   Yes   No

Credit Card   Yes   No

If Credit Card then state: Account No...

Expiry Date:..

Signature:..

Fee attached *(See page 102 for plan prices.)*   *Eur/£*..

Send all details to: **MK HOME DESIGN LTD.,**
22 Upper Patrick Street, Kilkenny, Ireland.
or Fax to 056-71300.

* A photocopy of this page is acceptable.